BOYS OF '72

LEEDS UNITED'S
FA CUP GLORY

BOYS OF '72

LEEDS UNITED'S
FA CUP GLORY

DAVID
SAFFER

TEMPUS

Nine of the Boys of '72 get together at a reunion. From left: Johnny Giles, Mick Bates, former coach Cyril Partridge, Eddie Gray, Norman Hunter, Allan Clarke, Jack Charlton, Paul Madeley, Peter Lorimer and Paul Reaney. Missing from the FA Cup winning team are Billy Bremner, David Harvey and Mick Jones.

First published 2005
Paperback edition first published 2006

Tempus Publishing Ltd
The Mill, Brimscombe Port
Stroud, Gloucestershire GL5 2QG
www.tempus-publishing.com

British Library Cataloguing in Publication Data.
A catalogue record for this book is available from the British Library.

ISBN 0 7524 3858 1

Typesetting and origination by Tempus Publishing
Printed and bound in Great Britain

Contents

Acknowledgements

Grateful thanks to the following people and organisations for their help with this publication: Don Warters, Mike Fisher at Yorkshire Post Newspapers Ltd, statistician Gary Shepherd and Holly Bennion at Tempus Publishing Ltd. Images for this publication have been supplied by Yorkshire Post Newspapers Ltd and Jack Hickes Photographers. Every effort has been made to identify the original source of other illustrations. For questions regarding copyright contact Tempus Publishing Ltd.

Lastly and most importantly, thanks to the Leeds United cup-winning team of 1972, together with the families of Don Revie and Billy Bremner, for reminiscing about a tremendous season in the club's history.

Foreword

Drinking beer out of t'owd tin pot – or to give it its Sunday name, the FA Cup – is an experience I shall never forget. I was at the after-match banquet in London a few hours after Allan Clarke's headed goal had given Leeds United a 1-0 victory over Arsenal in the centenary FA Cup final. The prestigious old trophy was being passed around delighted guests and I couldn't wait to get my hands on it. As I did so, something Don Revie had said to me a couple of years earlier came flooding back: 'Teams as good as the one we've got come round only once in a lifetime, so enjoy it while you can,' he told me.

Anyone who was fortunate enough to follow the fortunes of Leeds United through the Revie era will never forget the experience. There were 'ups' and 'downs' along the way, but one of the most joyous happenings for me was the season in which Leeds United won the FA Cup. That was the culmination of an impressive history-making campaign, one that I had followed so intently in my role as football correspondent of the *Yorkshire Evening Post*. Most would regard the league championship as a true indication of a team's ability because it tests players over a nine-month period, and there is a great deal of merit in that, but there is nothing quite like the excitement and tension that winning the FA Cup brings. It was the FA Cup I most wanted to see Leeds win in this particular season and I made the point in one of my pre-season articles. As things panned out, I wasn't to be disappointed.

It proved to be a season of memories, though unfortunately not all of them were good ones. Revie's team was at the height of its power and it made light of the Football Association's decision to punish the club by closing Elland Road for the first four home games of the season following crowd trouble during the previous campaign. After playing on neutral grounds where they won two and drew two, United returned to Elland Road and succeeded to make it a hell for opponents as they dropped only two points from their remaining 17 home games. Among those home games was the never-to-be-forgotten 7-0 thrashing of Southampton, the magic of which was captured on television, and also a 5-1 hammering of Manchester United in the previous game. No longer could Leeds be labelled boring and the headlines changed dramatically to 'Super Leeds'. They were indeed good times.

But the 1971/72 season should have been even more memorable for Leeds. It should have been a cup and league double-winning campaign, but United, despite their protests, were ordered by the Football League to play their final league game of the season at Wolves just forty-eight hours after the FA Cup final. What a ludicrous decision. It meant the United players could not celebrate their FA Cup win, as they had to travel to their Midlands base for the game at Molineux, which sadly they lost 2-1 and missed out on the title.

United and their followers had the FA Cup though. Allan Clarke's goal, which won the final, was something special. But the other memory I had of that Wembley day was the sight of the injured Mick Jones, his arm in a sling and his face etched in agony as, helped by teammate Norman Hunter, he slowly climbed the steps leading up to the Royal Box at Wembley to receive his winners' medal from the Queen. Painful though it obviously was for Mick, for me, his steely determination to get there typified the spirit Revie's talented side had displayed in their FA Cup-winning season. Leeds had never before won this most-coveted of domestic cup competitions and I was delighted for the manager, players and supporters.

Don Warters

Introduction

During Leeds United's eighty-six-year history, one era stands out. It started inauspiciously when Don Revie accepted the managerial reins in 1961. However, by the time of his departure thirteen years later, standards had been set that future teams would endeavour to chase. Managers and players have come and gone but all have played in the shadow of Revie's aces.

Prior to the Revie era, all United had to show for their efforts in terms of honours was a Second Division title in 1923/24, successful promotion campaigns in 1927/28, 1931/32 and 1955/56, and an FA Cup quarter-final appearance in 1950. After Revie's appointment the club's fortunes changed spectacularly. Winning the First Division twice, the FA Cup, the League Cup and two Fairs Cup titles, more major honours than any other English side between 1965 and 1974, Leeds United were feared domestically and throughout Europe.

For all the successes though, there were five First Division, three FA Cup, Fairs Cup and European Cup Winners' Cup runners-up spots as honours slipped away. However, despite the disappointments, Leeds United was the team to beat every season and, like a vintage bottle of port, time has enriched their legacy. Today, Revie and his squad are recognised as among the finest club sides the British game has known.

Revie managed Leeds in the First Division during a decade when numerous sides shared domestic trophies. Indeed, only Arsenal claimed the double during this period, a stark contrast to the past decade when the Gunners and Manchester United have achieved the feat on four occasions. It was an era when there was tremendous competition at the highest level. Every team had stars and it was impossible to predict the top two places before a season's opening games. Among a host of memories that Leeds enjoyed, the 1971/72 season epitomised Revie's tenure at the club. In a campaign that included triumph and tragedy aplenty, one date, one match and one moment stands out as iconic.

The date 6 May is the birthday of actor Orson Welles, baseball star Willie Mays and British prime minister Tony Blair. It is also a day in history when great deeds have been achieved. Inventor M.A. Cherry patented the tricycle in 1886, Roger Bannister became the first man to run a mile in less than four minutes in 1954, while President Eisenhower signed the Civil Rights Act of 1960. In 1972, 6 May was not notable in global terms, but for Leeds United supporters it will always live in the memory because Revie's legendary side defeated Arsenal in the FA Cup final at Wembley, clinching the trophy for the only time in the club's history. As for Allan Clarke's flying header, it is the most celebrated goal in club folklore.

The clash came at the end of a season when a Football Association ban meant Leeds had to play their opening four home League fixtures on neutral ground. The disadvantage was due to a pitch invasion at Elland Road by home supporters after referee Ray Tinkler allowed the most controversial offside goal ever witnessed at the ground, against lowly West Brom, towards the end of the previous campaign. Leeds lost the title by one point. The ban would haunt them in the dying embers of the 1971/72 league season. Revie's team had recovered from a slow start to be in the running for the league and cup double. However, after claiming the FA Cup, they were forced by football's authorities to play their final league fixture forty-eight hours after the victory against Arsenal. A 2-1 defeat at Wolves, when outrageous refereeing decisions affected the outcome, cost the much-coveted double.

More than three decades on, followers of the club and historians eulogise at the quality of football Revie's side displayed, especially in the second half of the campaign. It was breathtaking and, speaking with stars of his side, they select this period as a time when the team was at its peak. No supporter will ever forget the 5-1 win against Manchester United, the 7-0 trouncing of Southampton, nor hard-fought wins against Liverpool and Tottenham Hotspur on the road to Wembley. Above all, though, what has stood the test of time is the manner of the victories. If Leeds had to battle they could; if they got the opportunity to entertain they did so in abundance.

Leeds United, 1971/72. From left to right, back row: Belfitt, Hunter, Sprake, Harvey, Jordan, Yorath. Middle row: Faulkner, Galvin, Jones, Madeley, Clarke, Charlton. Front row: Reaney, Bates, Lorimer, Giles, Bremner (captain), Davey, Cooper.

Billy promotes his latest book with help from his friends.

Billy Bremner, Jack Charlton, Norman Hunter, Johnny Giles, Paul Reaney, Peter Lorimer et al were facing world stars every week such as Bobby Charlton, George Best, Bobby Moore, Geoff Hurst, Martin Peters, Alan Ball, Gordon Banks, Colin Bell, Francis Lee and Kevin Keegan. Every team had legendary personalities but Revie's boys were a match for them all.

This, then, is the backdrop to *Boys of '72*. It was a year when the *Evening Post* and a first-class stamp cost 3p, the average price of a loaf of white sliced bread was 9p, while a pint of milk, the *Radio Times* and an official Leeds United matchday programme all cost 5p. Popular football magazines such as *Scorcher* and *Score* cost 4p, *Shoot!* 6p and *Goal* 9p. The average price of a three-bedroom semi was £7,373 and a season ticket to watch Leeds United set supporters back anywhere between £1 and

£5. In an era when books on Leeds United were few and far between, four titles made the bookshelves during Christmas 1971: *The Leeds United Story* by Jason Thomas at £1.75, *Leeds United Book Of Football No.3* and *Billy Bremner's Book of Football* for the princely sum of £1 and *The Charlton Brothers* at £1.50 by Norman Harris.

Boys of '72 includes memories from the Leeds United squad in the 1972 FA Cup final together with comments by Don Revie and Billy Bremner by kind permission from their families. The search for original articles and memorabilia has been exhaustive. Of course, it is impossible to reproduce everything but the illustrations included express the mood, look and feel of the era. *Boys of '72* will bring back countless memories for fans who witnessed Revie's legendary side play, and for those who didn't, they will discover what pundits and personalities of the day observed.

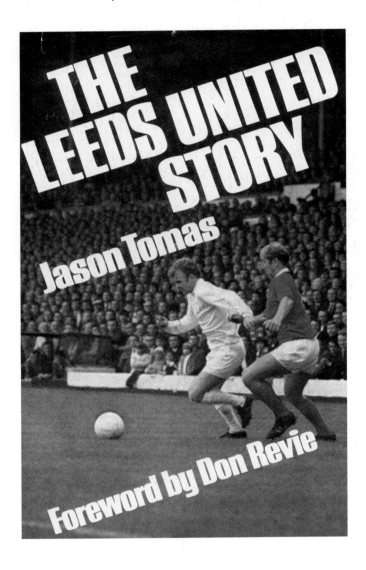

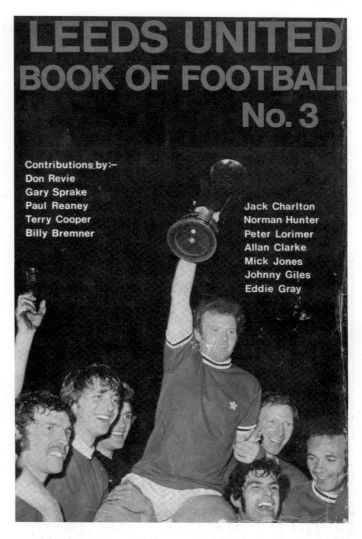

LEEDS UNITED
BOOK OF FOOTBALL
No. 3

Contributions by:—
Don Revie
Gary Sprake
Paul Reaney
Terry Cooper
Billy Bremner

Jack Charlton
Norman Hunter
Peter Lorimer
Allan Clarke
Mick Jones
Johnny Giles
Eddie Gray

For me, this campaign has always been special. At twelve years of age, Leeds United was a major part of my life and I recall all the highs and lows of an unforgettable season. The FA Cup success that term, unbeknown to me, would start my writing career and I will forever feel linked to the events of a remarkable campaign when the Gaffer (Revie), Suave (Harvey), Speedy (Reaney), Big Ed (Madeley), Top Cat (Cooper), Chalky (Bremner), Big Jack (Charlton), Bites yer Legs (Hunter), Lasher (Lorimer), Sniffer (Clarke), Jonah (Jones), Farmer (Giles) and Last Waltz (Gray) ruled the roost.

Enjoy the memories.

David Saffer
6 May 2005

LEEDS UNITED back in action!

One of those white-hot moments which are the essence of Soccer — Leeds United skipper Billy Bremner hovers over Chelsea 'keeper Peter Bonetti, hoping for a half-chance. Picture by Irvine Crawford.

The EVENING POST kicks off with a winner

Inside: Full colour souvenir wall chart

1

Ready for Action

When Leeds United's squad assembled for pre-season training in July 1971, the usual buzz enveloped Elland Road. Paul Reaney recalls:

'When you have been away for a few weeks you miss the banter. Football is all about banter, whether you are in the dressing room, training or about to play a game and you miss that. Mickey-takers – Johnny Giles was a nightmare, as was Billy Bremner. Sniffer Clarke was very shrewd and knew exactly what he was doing. Most picked-on was Jonah. He was quiet but a great lad. You could do anything to Jonah and he definitely got the most stick. It was all harmless fun though and helped to generate the team spirit we had. Most of us had arrived at Leeds as youngsters on the ground staff. We grew up together and knew each other inside out, which created morale and meant we would fight for each other. We felt that we were peaking because games roll onto you. You're so fit, games were easier than training; it's no effort. When players complained they were shattered after forty games it amazed me because we used to go on and on, and moaned if we were not playing because Don always played his best side. We knew from an early age what Don wanted and respected him totally; we were all in it together. Don was sometimes called lucky because of the quality players at Leeds but he brought them all to the club. He got as close to us as we did to him. Don looked after us like a second father and that is what made it. We would sweat blood for the gaffer. Every season the target was that we were not going to lose a game. We were in every competition, sometimes to our cost because when you play so many games and go for everything you start to get a bit weary when the semi-finals and finals occur. Of course there is pressure because you are at the latter stages of the league and you do not like losing semi-finals; the extremes of a winning and loosing dressing room is incredible. Perhaps that was a problem but it's very difficult to say you are only going for one competition because if you get knocked out of that you have nothing. You have to go for everything and see where you are at the end. The 1971/72 campaign was like any other. We went out to win every competition.'

For supporters, as the build-up occurred, two results from the previous campaign rankled. Both, a shock FA Cup fifth round defeat at Fourth Division Colchester United and a heartbreaking defeat by West Brom that ultimately cost the title, are among the most infamous in the club's history. Upon drawing Colchester in the FA Cup, Leeds sat top of the First Division. Nobody gave Colchester a chance. Barry Foster in the *Yorkshire Post* described Leeds as the 'giant in the biggest giant-killing act since Jack and the Beanstalk'. In arguably the competition's greatest upset the underdogs prevailed with a 3-2 victory.

LEEDS UNITED FOOTBALL CLUB
OFFICIAL HANDBOOK

1972   10p

Essential pre-season reading for United supporters.

Paul Madeley:

'No excuses, they deserved their win. Apart from Billy everyone was there, it was a big disappointment but that's what the FA Cup is all about and why it is so special. Tactically we made mistakes, which was unusual for us. Don mistakenly thought that due to the bumpy pitch we'd be unable to play our normal passing game. We gave the ball away a lot and consequently suffered. We were indecisive at the back and found ourselves 3-0 down, which no one could quite believe. We came back with goals from Norman and Johnny when we played our regular game but it was too late. We ran out of time for one of the great cup shocks. The papers had a field day.'

Norman Hunter:

'I remember walking out with the Big Jack. The pitch was a bit hard and windy and I said to Jack that this was going to be hard work. To be fair they started well but Gary had a poor game. As a defender, you want your 'keeper to be certain with his calls. Simmons and Crawford could not believe their luck because Gary was so unsure. He'd say "mine Norm, no yours," it was unbelievable. We were 3-0 down and deservedly so. We got it back to 3-2 and had twenty minutes to equalise but could not do it. Colchester's 'keeper made a great save late on but that's the beauty of the FA Cup and it made the whole country very happy. I've seen the video since. They played way above their station, played some good stuff and deserved the win. People talk about giant-killing; that was some result.'

Leeds sat top of the league when they faced West Brom at Elland Road in the penultimate home game of the season. Jeff Astle scored the Baggies' controversial second goal in a 2-1 victory. BBC *Match of the Day* cameras covered the game refereed by Ray Tinkler and analysed key moments with slow-motion replays. Three decades on Astle's tap-in is still one of the most talked-about incidents of the era. At the time, commentator Barry Davies exclaimed: 'And Leeds will go mad! And they have every right to go mad!' His words echoed Leeds supporters' feelings. Don Revie commented bitterly on television that nine months' hard work was down the drain by a referee's decision. As for Tinkler, he was adamant that the key player at the centre of the controversy, Colin Suggett, was not interfering with play. Tinkler required a police escort after the game and never officiated at Elland Road again. Leeds players still recall the incident clearly. Allan Clarke:

'When Tony Brown intercepted Norman's pass and broke across the halfway line, the linesman immediately raised his flag as Suggett was clearly offside. We all stopped but Tinkler waved play on. Brown raced forward before squaring for Astle, also looking offside, to roll the ball into an empty net. The crowd erupted, the lads and gaffer protested but Tinkler was adamant. My goal was consolation. Tinkler cost us the title. In the dressing room we went crackers. It was the worst refereeing decision of my career.'

The pitch invasion resulted in the Football Association banning Leeds from playing their opening four home games at Elland Road. The club felt hard done by and

Hard work!

received media sympathy, but for the players it was business as usual. Norman Hunter:

'We all had our own thoughts about the ban. So did Don, but he kept those away from us. "There was nothing we could do about it," he said, "that's done. We start again next season." It's only now when you look back over the records and you realise that we were badly done. You can't go on about it because people say its sour grapes.'

Paul Reaney:

'The result rankled a bit but it was over. We could not change the result, it was a big disappointment to us but you can't reflect on that. Another season was upon us and you had to get on with it.'

The Football Association ban was the most written-about subject in the media during the build-up to the new campaign, with pundits debating whether it was harsh or not and whether it would affect the team's chances of silverware in 1971/72.

Different magazines had their own opinions. In *Goal*, Robert Holmes assessed each First Division club's chances of success. Holmes predicted Liverpool would win the Championship, with Derby County the dark horses, while Manchester United, Spurs and West Brom would be good bets in the FA Cup. As for Leeds United, Holmes predicted a tough season.

LEEDS: Seasons at the top, under a great strain, have understandably taken their toll of Don Revie's battle-hardened warriors. Unless he can call up fresh reserves, Revie might be near his Waterloo. GOALcast: The last throes of a great team.

Chris Davies of *Shoot!* was not so pessimistic. He believed that Revie's side would still be the team to beat:

Financially, the club will lose thousands of pounds, but in soccer at the top, where money is no object, I'm sure Leeds will not worry too much as long as their early season results away from home are favourable. So, Leeds will kick off the season with eight 'away' games. On the face of it, this is a major problem but looking deeper Leeds have little to fear. In the past three seasons Leeds have lost only eight away games. No other club can claim such an impressive record in the world's toughest division. Don Revie told me: 'To be honest, we find we play better away from home. We're allowed more room. So many teams come to Elland Road and shut up shop with eight or nine men in defence.' Now the closure of Elland Road seems to be

Instruction: Don lays down team tactics.

less drastic than it may have appeared at first. If Leeds can manage twelve points from those eight 'away' games, they will have done magnificently and how many people would be brave enough to say it's beyond Leeds? The bookmakers, notorious for being miserly with their odds, will offer no more than odds of 4-1 against Leeds winning the title next season. Leeds may not be Champions, but their reputation is such that they are still the team everyone loves to beat. A victory over Leeds is a great boost for any club, but this is something the Yorkshire side have learned to live with. Too professional, that's the key to Leeds' present position and it must be remembered also that they are still a young side, most of their players are either at or approaching their peak. Players like Clarke, Cooper, Hunter still only in their mid-twenties. So don't write off Leeds, ban or no ban!

Looking ahead to the campaign, Billy Bremner noted:

'We are a vastly experienced side and have the ability and enthusiasm necessary to sustain a bold bid throughout this season, even taking into account the extra 'away' matches in the league. Pre-season training has gone very well at Elland Road. Although we have had a break from football, lasting only six weeks, the lads have been very keen and I think the closure of our ground is going to make them all the more determined to do well this season. There is an air of confidence about the place.'

Allan Clarke spoke with Ray Bradley of *Goal*. Asked whether Leeds were past their best, the sharpshooter said:

'You must be joking. We finished second in the league last year. We won the Fairs Cup against some of the best opposition in Europe. Does that sound as if we are past our best? Personally, I don't think we have reached our peak. You need a bit of luck to win anything today. Without taking anything away from Arsenal's fine achievement I think that they had that little bit of luck that clinched the title. This season I think they'll find it harder, they'll find out what life at the top is all about. Arsenal will feel the pressure just as we did. A draw against them will be considered a great result. Everyone will be going all out to beat them and that suits us fine.'

Regarding the League campaign, Clarke noted:

'We shall be as determined as ever. It's no secret that the boss would like us to win the title again and we're all behind him. We want to have another crack at the European Cup again, but we shall take each match as it comes. Team spirit at Elland Road couldn't be better. We'll all be in there pulling for each other. We don't know the meaning of the word defeat.'

As for a goals target, he commented:

'I don't believe in setting targets. I just go out each game and try to get as many as I can. I managed to get 24 goals last season and I'll be happy to equal that number again. If I happen to improve on that then I'll be even happier. Goals are hard to come by and they get harder to score every season. Leeds did seventy per cent of the attacking in most games last season, but

it doesn't ease the problem. You still find the penalty area packed. People say, "That was a good goal" or "That was an easy one." As far as I am concerned all goals are good goals as long as they count.'

Asked whether life is tough as a striker, Clarke responded:

'It's not easy. It never has been. Perhaps it becomes harder every season, but I never consciously think about it on the field. I've got a job to do and I try to do it to the best of my ability. Sometimes the fans expect miracles. They expect you to score in every game. It's not that easy; sometimes they go in, sometimes they don't. I'm only human; I don't expect to take all my chances. I've learned to take the rough with the smooth. I suppose I'm lucky really to have a partner like Mick Jones. In my book Mick's a great player. He takes a lot of knocks and never complains. Playing alongside him has helped me a lot. I also like to think I've helped him. Mick plays farther up front; I play deeper, but our aims are the same; to score as many goals as we can for Leeds.'

Malcolm Allison (Manchester City assistant manager) described Clarke as the finest finisher in the game; coldly efficient and completely nerveless around the box. Clarke says:

'I don't think of myself as coldly efficient. Maybe I don't show my true feelings because this is part of my character. I just build myself up for every match. From Thursday I key myself up. Completely nerveless? Mal must be joking. From schoolboy days I've had a knack of scoring goals. Most of them are the result of instinctive reaction. I've trained myself to be alert around the box. Sometimes you run away from a defender to gain that vital split second; you may get the ball in an open space, you may not, but you've got to be alert in case the chance comes. It's just as hard for me as anyone else.'

In another feature, Bradley rated Paul Madeley 'pound for pound' the most valuable professional in the First Division. Madeley told Bradley:

'I've been a pro eight years but only a regular for three. I've learned to be patient and have not been out of the side for the past two seasons except for injuries, so being adaptable has obviously proved an asset in my case. Although as a professional I'm always prepared to play where I'm picked, I personally prefer to play in midfield because, in addition to being in the game more, you have a freer role. I'll play for Leeds anywhere they want me, that's the way we've been brought up at Elland Road, "all for one and one for all". As for this season, I would really like to see Leeds win the FA Cup. Winning the cup is personally my biggest ambition.'

Journalists up and down the country shared Davies' optimism. The spirit in the camp was excellent. The squad had grown up together, were used to adversity and pulled on their experiences from past seasons when they had bounced back from disappointments. Lining up for team photographs, they were not without silverware following their Fairs Cup triumph against Italian giants Juventus on away goals. The *Boys of '72* were ready for action.

Looking to the future, teenage reserve striker Joe Jordan featured in a *Goal* article. Jordan said:

'Although most of my football at Elland Road has been in the reserve side, after being a first-team player with Morton, I am quite happy with my progress with Leeds. They are a wonderful club and the set-up is really professional. They go out of their way to make sure every new player feels at home. Every effort is made to get the best out of each player and I go back in the afternoons for special training sessions. I really feel the benefit. I realise that I may have to wait for some time before I get the opportunity to establish myself in the first team. No young striker can expect to displace stars like Allan Clarke, Mick Jones and Rod Belfitt overnight. My aim is to gain experience in the reserve side and be ready to prove myself when the chance arises. I think the club will be in the running for honours again next season. With players like Billy Bremner, Johnny Giles, Clarke, Eddie Gray and Peter Lorimer and so many other stars Leeds can hardly fail to do well, provided they get a fair share of the breaks. The team spirit is so good here, there are no big-heads and everyone helps each other out.'

In the *Evening Post* pre-season special, correspondents predicted an exciting season. Don Warters noted:

Ask any professional soccer player for his views on the coming season and it is a safe bet that he will put Leeds United well to the fore in his list for honours once more. United have been among the 'chosen few' for several seasons now and understandably too, for they have proved to be one of the most consistently good sides in the country... I would like to see United win the FA Cup, a trophy they have never won. Players, it is said, derive a greater satisfaction from winning the League, a pointer to consistency in 42 games played over a period of nine months in varied conditions, but for pure glory the FA Cup cannot be beaten. In a nutshell, the season ahead is one to look forward to with confidence.

2

The Marathon Begins

Leeds kicked off the new campaign with a hard-fought victory at Manchester City, Peter Lorimer's striking providing the cutting edge. Paul Doherty (*The People*) commented:

Leeds have begun yet another season's exhaustive course in the grand manner. Lorimer proved to be the one special cutting edge, which divided the teams.

Somewhat surprisingly though, a 3-0 defeat against Sheffield United, a bad-tempered encounter that saw the Blades wrap-up victory with two goals in the final three minutes, heralded a run that saw Revie's team suffer more losses in the opening ten league games than in the whole of previous season. Following the defeat at Bramall Lane, Billy Bremner said:

'People seem to take a delight in knocking Leeds but I can assure all our fans that we are far from finished. I have never seen the lads so grimly determined. We want to show everyone that we are still very much alive. Despite the fact that we have had to play four "home" games away from Elland Road, we shall still be there or thereabouts at the end of the season.'

Jack Charlton added:

'There isn't a team in the country who could go into a match with a seventy per cent chance of beating us. We are still the team to beat and I can't see why anyone should doubt our quality. It's still us and somebody else who'll be fighting it out for the league title.'

Of the four 'home' matches played there were disappointing draws against Wolves and Tottenham Hotspur and victories against Newcastle United and Crystal Palace. Top scorers the previous season, Bremner's goal in a 1-1 draw with Tottenham was welcome relief as Leeds had notched just one goal in 270 minutes of football. The 5-1 win against the Geordies was far more encouraging. Derek Wallis (*Daily Mirror*):

Leeds captivated the crowd with the quality of their football, notably in midfield, where Giles and Bremner captured the imagination. The pick of Leeds' goals was Charlton's opener, executed straight from the training ground, set up brilliantly by Giles and Reaney... It could hardly have been better planned had it been the thousandth performance in a live theatre. Certainly it deserved a far bigger audience than Hillsborough provided.

Official
Programme 5p

LEEDS UNITED
versus Wolverhampton Wanderers

Saturday, 21st August, 1971   Kick-off 3 p.m.
at LEEDS ROAD, Huddersfield

Leeds United

Colours :
WHITE SHIRTS, WHITE SHORTS

1. GARY SPRAKE
2. PAUL REANEY
3. TERRY COOPER
4. BILLY BREMNER
5. JACK CHARLTON
6. NORMAN HUNTER
7. PETER LORIMER
8. ALAN CLARKE
9. ROD BELFITT
10. JOHNNY GILES
11. PAUL MADELEY

Sub. ....

Wolves

Colours :
GOLD SHIRTS, BLACK SHORTS

1. PHILIP PARKES
2. BERNARD SHAW
3. DEREK PARKINS
4. MICHAEL BAILEY
5. FRANCIS MUNRO
6. JOHN McALLE
7. JIM McCALLIOG
8. KENNETH HIBBITT
9. ROBERT GOULD
10. DEREK DOUGAN
11. DAVID WAGSTAFFE

Sub. ....

REFEREE :
Mr. R. L. JOHNSON, Lowestoft
LINESMEN :
Mr. B. HEALEY, Northwich
RED FLAG
Mr. D. ROGERS, Derby
YELLOW FLAG

Despite missing a number of regulars, the opening games were proving a torrid experience for Revie's charges. Apart from their 'home' fixtures, Leeds were also struggling on genuine travels. After an encouraging 2-0 win at Ipswich Town, a much-awaited clash at defending champions Arsenal ended in disappointment, although Leeds were shorn of Sprake, Cooper, Jones and Gray. Mike Langley (*The People*) wrote off any hopes of silverware for Leeds this term:

Don Revie squirmed through a grim afternoon in the glass-fronted trainers' box, hunched, chewing incessantly and peering into a worrying future. For he could only see another season of comparative failure for Leeds United, the team that for the past two seasons have always stumbled in second. This time, on this form, they probably won't even do that.

Tony Pawson (*Observer*):

About the only thing Arsenal could not do last season was to win a game against Leeds, so this victory was all the sweeter. But Leeds without Cooper are a little like gin without the tonic.

Another Madeley goal, this time against Crystal Palace at Leeds' 'home' venue Leeds Road, Huddersfield.

Jordan (8) wheels away after scoring against Barcelona.

Things didn't get better following a 2-1 defeat at lowly Huddersfield Town. Keith Macklin (*The People*):

Like the pugnacious terrier who likes nothing better than to bait the Alsatian, Town's terriers made light of form and enthusiasm.

Notwithstanding Bremner and Charlton's comments, the opening months of the season saw Leeds crash out of the UEFA Cup to Norwegian minnows Lierse SK, their only previous European encounter an 8-0 aggregate defeat to Manchester City, and the League Cup to West Ham. Leeds also lost a Fairs Cup play-off against Barcelona 2-1 for the right to keep the old Fairs Cup. Playing weakened teams in both legs of a 4-2 aggregate defeat to Lierse SK (Leeds won the opening leg in Norway 2-0), missing Sprake, Charlton, Hunter, Bremner, Giles, Clarke, Jones and Gray in the Elland Road tie, the Leeds boss denied his side had been complacent. Revie told Derek Potter (*The Express*):

'We did not underestimate them. We have no excuses and now we have got to get down to it again. This was the best team I could play in the circumstances.'

Asked if Leeds had 'opted out' of Europe by a *Yorkshire Evening Post* reporter, Revie gave a terse response:

'It is absolute nonsense to suggest we deliberately chose to go out of this European competition. We never opt out of anything. In fact, it will be recalled that we have been criticised in the past

for taking on so much. At the beginning of this season, I made it clear that we would have a go for everything we entered for. There has been no change in policy. Anyone who thinks we opted out is thinking entirely along the wrong lines.'

Inconsistent form had been at the root of United's problems. Allan Clarke and Mick Jones were struggling with knocks and Eddie Gray's absence meant Paul Madeley switched from right-back to the anchor role in midfield, enabling Paul Reaney to return into the fold. Also missing for a brief spell was skipper Billy Bremner, following an injury sustained against Derby County in a League Cup clash. This was his fourth injury of the year and summed up a frustrating period when he missed much of the 1970/71 campaign. He was absent when Leeds lost to Colchester United and only returned for the latter stages of the Fairs Cup triumph, even though clearly not fully fit. His injury against Derby meant he was sidelined for a clash at Coventry City. Prior to the fixture James Mossop (*Sunday Express*) interviewed the Leeds talisman:

When he's playing football the squawking, flapping, scurrying Billy Bremner looks like a little red rooster amok in a chicken run. But this weekend he sits in a corner with his wings clipped. He looks up at the huge dressing room sign, which implores everyone to 'Keep Fighting' and sighs a high of helplessness. Bremner says: 'I saw Archie Gemmill's boot coming over and I

Belgium blues!

just checked out. He still caught me full on. I thought my leg was broken until I looked down. He had gone through everything so I could see for myself that the bone was still intact. It was only that that stopped me fainting. Archie came over to me on the touchline and said "I'm sorry about that wee man." I told him not to worry and we had a beer afterwards. That's what I mean about hazards of the trade. If you fell out over these things you wouldn't have a friend left. It's sickening because I had felt right before it. Last season I had ankle, groin and knee troubles and finally a hairline fracture. I never seemed able to get properly fit. Sometimes it hurts and you are made to look slow, but there is not a player here who wouldn't play if the boss (Don Revie) asked him. That's the sort of club it is. Not being able to play kills me; I can't bear to watch the lads. I want to be out there, involved. So I sit at home watching television trying to keep my mind off the game. But I'm like an ostrich. I want to bury my head and I also want to know what's happening. I want most of all to be doing my bit on the field, especially with so many other players injured.' Leeds United need Bremner's indomitable courage. The 'wee man', as footballers call him, is the most gutsy, zealous footballer I know. He is a wing half of insatiable drive. His skills are rich but above all he drains himself in every match. He is one man who does not need that 'Keep Fighting' sign.

Out of sorts, Leeds crashed 3-1. The defeat that saw Revie's team slip to ninth place, six points behind new pacesetters Manchester United. Eric Nicholls (*The People*):

Cool, calculated and classy Coventry ripped into Leeds and tore enough holes in their back division to send Revie away with a king-sized headache.

Another reporter noted:

Not only did cock-a-hoop Coventry beat Leeds yesterday for the first time ever, they positively took them to the cleaners. Don Revie hurried away from Highfield Road under police escort. No-one could have blamed Revie as he rushed away to escape this humiliation. His Leeds Lions were reduced to toothless cubs.

Fortunately for the Leeds captain, this would be his only period out during the season. A return to form was always on the cards when players regained fitness and so it proved when Clarke and Jones returned for their first league game together against Manchester City in the next fixture. The match was Leeds' first appearance on the BBC's *Match of the Day* programme during the campaign and both scored in a 3-0 win that saw Leeds make strides up the table, back up to sixth spot, six points behind the Old Trafford team chasing a first title since 1967/68. Clarke announced his return when he pounced on a slight hesitation in the visitors' defence, ghosting between two defenders before coolly drilling home a splendid goal. Jones scored a clinical close-range volley but picked up another injury. The match was also notable for a sensational thirty-yard strike from 'Hot Shot' Lorimer in the last minute. Len Swift (*The People*):

Don Revie promised that Leeds would be as dangerous as ever once they had cleared their injury pile-up and £265,000 strike twins Allan Clarke and Mick Jones were as good as their

Nº 10453

LEEDS UNITED A.F.C. TOKEN

MAN. CITY
10
1971-72

Official Programme 5p

LEEDS UNITED
versus MANCHESTER CITY

Saturday, 16th October, 1971
at ELLAND ROAD, Leeds

Kick-off 3 p.m.

REFEREE :
Mr. W. J. GOW, Swansea
LINESMEN :
Mr. D. RICHARDSON, Blackburn
RED FLAG
Mr. R. HODGSON, Houghton-le-Spring
YELLOW FLAG

Leeds United
Colours :
WHITE SHIRTS, WHITE SHORTS
1. GARY SPRAKE
2. PAUL REANEY
3. TERRY COOPER
4. BILLY BREMNER
5. JACK CHARLTON
6. NORMAN HUNTER
7. PETER LORIMER
8. TERRY YORATH
9. ROD BELFITT
10. JOHNNY GILES
11. PAUL MADELEY

Sub...

Manchester City
Colours :
SKY BLUE SHIRTS, WHITE SHORTS
1. JOE CORRIGAN
2. TONY BOOK
3. DAVID CONNOR
4. MICHAEL DOYLE
5. TOMMY BOOTH
6. TONY TOWERS
7. MIKE SUMMERBEE
8. WILLIE DONACHIE
9. NEIL YOUNG
10. FRANCIS LEE
11. IAN MELLOR

Sub...

Jones fires home against Manchester City.

boss' word. This was Leeds back at their commanding and menacing best, moving the ball about quickly and accurately, tackling like tanks and always running but never on the run.

Lorimer's strike received much publicity. Ray Bradley (*Goal*) said his thunderbolt demonstrated he had few peers in the art of volleying a moving ball and illustrated clearly he could mix skill and subtlety with stunning power when the occasion demanded. Lorimer said:

'When I received the ball from Billy Bremner, Willie Donachie was tight on me. I flicked it over him and managed to catch it right on the volley. I suppose it was as good a goal as I have ever scored but it doesn't matter how you score them; they all count if they cross the line.'

Back on track, Billy Bremner gave forthright views about the mixed results in an in-depth interview with Eric Nicholls (*Goal*). Asked whether Leeds were now back on song following the City victory, he said:

'I certainly hope so. Don't forget we've had a lot of injuries but I've got to be honest there was more to it than that. Ability-wise were still very good but we were content to play with the ball. We weren't winning it often enough when the other side had it. We had to get this right. We were concerned about it and had lots of discussions in small groups and as a team and I hope we have sorted it out.'

On his telepathic partnership with Johnny Giles he noted:

'When you have played together for so long you develop this understanding. Johnny and I have been together for six years now. He is a tremendous little thinker and he is always in the right position to receive a pass. This makes it easier for anyone to play with him.'

As for targets the Leeds skipper said:

'We believe in going for the lot but obviously the league championship is the big one. People talk about the strain of chasing too many pots. What strain? I've never known any. When you are having a good run it gets you so you can't wait for the next game to come around. I could never understand all the talk in newspapers about the strain we were supposed to be under when we were chasing the treble.'

Regarding Leeds' chances of winning the double, Bremner commented:

'When you have been at the top for a while you get to be a team like, say, the Busby Babes were. I'm not trying to compare us with that great side but like us, they were successful. That means everyone is out to beat you. With respect to Arsenal, they are only just learning what it's like to be at the top. All credit to them, they won the double fair and square but they didn't have the rest of the league gunning for them.'

Finally, on the subject of his share of injuries and rumours that he was on the way out, he said:

'Right now I'm fitter than I have ever been and I'm enjoying my game more because I've increased my work rate. I'm more determined to win things and I'll tell you this, Billy Bremner is far from finished.'

Backing Bremner to the full was Don Revie. Discussing his skipper's impact in *Goal* magazine, the Leeds boss said:

'Respect is the main thing, but a skipper has got to have ability. He must be brave, courageous in the tackle. He must run for ninety minutes. Bremner has all these qualities; he's a truly great player. He learned a lot about skippering while playing with people like Bobby Collins and Jack Charlton, and Johnny Giles has always been there to help. Bremner is a fine example to all others. He wouldn't ask any of them to do something he couldn't do. On top of all this, he has this tremendous will to win. He is a great skipper.'

A 3-2 win at home against Everton, summed-up by Barry Foster (*Yorkshire Post*) as a match that 'might not be for the connoisseur', was followed by a 1-0 victory at league leaders Manchester United. The result, courtesy of a Peter Lorimer strike, narrowed the gap to just four points as Leeds moved into the top four for the first time. *The People's* correspondent noted:

The match was never the spectacle it had promised to be simply because Leeds, once they go in front, intend to hold supremacy, and Manchester, their rhythm gone, resorted to tactics that should have no place in a side that prides itself on being one of England's showpiece performers... Leeds, so assured, so much in command, played 'keepball' and for the first time this season Manchester were completely out-manoeuvred in the middle of the field.

Journalist Bob Hughes noted:

Mature, purposeful professionalism is still able to overcome virtuosity of the highest order. The goal from Lorimer was speculative and fortunate, but the victory was one of vastly superior purpose and organisation. The advantage was comprehensively conceived and deservedly defended by a team of true championship pretensions. Leeds were busier, quicker (particularly off the ball) and as selfless as usual in their running for each other.

Lorimer's fourth-minute strike was labelled a 'freak', but not by the goalscorer himself. Lorimer said:

'The way it looked on TV, Alex made a mess up of my shot but it wasn't like that. It's hard on him to say he should have stopped it. If he had it would have been a fine save. First of all Alex must have had a terrible time picking up the line of the shot. I'm not saying it was a wonderful drive but I didn't mis-hit and certainly it swerved over the last ten yards. From the moment I saw it turn I knew it would be a goal. Alex was going the wrong way. I know that when you hit this type of ball, inevitably it swerves.'

Both Clarke and Jones finally returned, following a last-gasp defeat at Southampton, forming part of a run of seven victories in eight games. Among the victories was a 2-1 home triumph against Leicester City. Coming from behind, Eddie Gray was the star, setting up goals for Bremner and Lorimer. Terry Brindle (*Yorkshire Post*):

Lose is a four-letter word at Elland Road; Leeds rolled up their sleeves and put Leicester under severe second half pressure. They had that overriding will to win, which has risen to greater challenges than this, and they had a winsome, mercurial match-winner in the shape of Eddie Gray.

The victory was welcome, but the news during the build-up and in the post-match coverage surrounded the collapse of Leeds' £177,000 purchase of twenty-one-year-old West Brom midfielder Asa Hartford after a medical revealed a hole in his heart. Hartford had even trained for his new teammates but his planned debut never materialised. Prior to the bombshell, Hartford told Don Warters (*Yorkshire Evening Post*):

'The transfer came as a terrific shock, but I have no worries about joining this terrific United squad. You get a chance once in a lifetime, you grab it with both hands. Now it is up to me not to waste the opportunity.'

Don Revie's first major signing since Allan Clarke for a British record fee in 1969, Revie told Frank Clough (*The Sun*):

'I have bought this boy to ensure our future. He is only twenty-one and I think he is in the same mould as Billy Bremner. He has at least ten years of top-class football in front of him. I have liked him for two years but I never thought he would become available. Not many great players come on to the market during a season, so when one comes along whom you rate, you have to go for

him. People may think we may be selling someone now that we have this boy. They are way out, our top-class players are staying here. Hartford is now a member of our first-team pool.'

Following the medical, a statement issued by United secretary and general manager Keith Archer read: 'The transfer of Asa Hartford from WBA to Leeds United has been called off owing to a medical condition. Any further statement must come from WBA.' West Brom secretary Alan Everiss said:

'Hartford played for us last Saturday and he trained during the week. I am informed that Don Revie is very upset about this as are we. I can imagine how Hartford must feel about all this, as he was looking forward to playing for Leeds. His world has turned completely over in twenty-four hours.'

Hartford went on to enjoy a fine career with the Midlanders, Manchester City and Scotland.

Away from the 'Hartford Affair', Leeds got back into the groove. Lorimer settled a clash against Stoke City, despite Gordon Banks being in imperious form, saving his side on countless occasions. Following a last-minute 2-1 defeat at Southampton, Leeds bounced back with a 2-0 win at Nottingham Forest. Defeated manager Matt Gillies told the *Express* that everything was back to normal at Leeds United:

'Make no mistake, Leeds are still the finest team in the country. They may have had their troubles early in the season but they are now showing real poise and assurance. They'll take some stopping.'

Hugh Johns (*The People*):

The slick professional skills of Leeds, every one of them a senior international, crushed Forest like matchwood, and two goals makes a mockery of the scoreline, it could have been seven.

Reporter Keith Macklin (*The People*) noted, after a 3-0 defeat at home to West Brom, Asa Hartford and all, that Leeds:

Stroked the ball about with such comfortable confidence, it smacked of disdain for their opponents.

Halfway through the League campaign, following a tasty 0-0 draw at Chelsea, Leeds sat third in the League, five points off the pace behind Manchester United and Manchester City. More than anything, Don Revie was delighted to have his twin strikers Allan Clarke and Mick Jones, and Eddie Gray back in the side. Speaking in *Goal*, the Leeds boss said:

It's tremendous to have them back in the side again. Naturally, when you have players like them out of the action you really miss them. They've had only a handful of games together this

Giles scores in Leeds' win over West Brom.

season and although the players who took over from them did a magnificent job, their experience means such a lot.

In their third season as a strike force the Clarke-Jones partnership was feared throughout Europe. In an article titled 'The Finishing Touch' (Marshall Cavendish), Revie said:

There is far more to their partnership than brawn and finishing power. They both have tremendous skill. I've rarely seen a man (Clarke) so quick to see a chance and take it. Leave a half-chance in the penalty area and Allan Clarke will turn it into a goal before you've realised he has the room. He and Mick Jones read each other perfectly. There are times when Mick doesn't get the credit he deserves but I doubt if there is a harder skilled worker in the whole of football.

On his role, Jones commented:

'I know just what I have to do, peg away at it. I have to keep going all the time, stirring things up whether or not there's a goal in it for me. Sometimes I think it's a good job I'm a placid kind of bloke, otherwise I could get in all sorts of trouble with referees when it gets rough. A lot of people talk about my being able to jump and hang in the air but there is no mystery about it. Any player who has normal heading ability can master the technique. It's simply a question of timing. You have to get up early, that's all, and once you've mastered it, the knack never leaves you.'

Clarke was quick to praise his partner:

'Mick's strength and stamina amaze me. He keeps running all through the season. With a player of his size and skill it makes things easier for me. You can bet that most times I score Mick will have played some part in it. I'm certain not enough football fans appreciate just how good a player Mick Jones is. He's not just a bulldozer, he has skill, intelligence and strength.'

As for his role, Clarke said:

'I'm sort of freelance. I'm allowed to go wherever I think there could be a chance or a half-chance. It's a case of sensing which is the right place. I can go up front from different angles, not always alongside Mick but a lot of it is understanding. We know each other's play inside out. We can tell what's going to happen no matter where each of us is.'

Looking back at the partnership, Mick says:

'Allan's arrival was the final piece of the team. Don always told me I was doing an excellent job but in Allan he spotted something different and we both gained from our partnership. We became friends off the field and it's a friendship that has lasted. He had a tag that he could be a problem-player but from his first day at the club he was nothing like the press made out. He found a group of players as ambitious as him and he settled immediately. It took a while to get a good understanding but once it developed we never collided because we were different types of players.'

Allan added:

'Jonah was the target-man and he led the line as well as anyone I ever played with or against. He also scored some tremendous goals. Although he wasn't six-foot tall he climbed better than anybody I'd ever seen. As for our partnership, he would hold the line and I'd go and look for the ball anywhere. If I was being man-marked I'd go back to the halfway line or even deeper to pick balls up. Any crosses that came into the box I always joined him. One of us would attack the near post, the other would peel off to the back stick. We blended perfectly and developed a telepathic understanding.'

Ominously Leeds were truly back in the title race. Johnny Giles, interviewed in *Goal*, commented:

'I don't think any one thing has suddenly made us tick. We started off this season still as good a team just as we finished last season but we have faced problems. We began by having to play our home games away; we had Allan Clarke, Mick Jones and Eddie Gray out of action through injury for lengthy spells. These are things that obviously don't help a side click into top gear. For instance, with Allan and Mick out, I was less inclined to venture upfield. It showed in the fact that I scored few goals. Last season I hit 13 in the League games, now with half a season gone I've scored only 5 (two penalties) but when your front runners are on the sidelines you don't feel inclined to take risks by going upfield, you want to keep things tight at the back. However, if our early setbacks did achieve something for us, it was the fact that, for a change, we weren't the pacemakers in the title race and this helped to take some of the pressure off us. So in one way it helped, even if we're used to pressure. Then we beat Manchester City after a bad defeat against Coventry. That win gave us an injection of

Lorimer fires home against Derby County.

Gray slots a goal against the Rams.

36

confidence and we carried on by beating Everton, Manchester United and Leicester. Before the Manchester United game at Old Trafford we were six points adrift, by the time we'd beaten Leicester we'd halved the gap and got ourselves tucked into a handy position. That United game was a handy one for us.'

By Christmas, Leeds found themselves five points adrift from the top in fourth spot after a 1-1 draw at Crystal Palace and a 3-0 defeat of high-flying Derby County. Although Lorimer grabbed a brace, including a twenty-five-yard special, the pick of Leeds' three goals was Eddie Gray's opener, neatly dispatched after a deft one-two between Bremner and his Scottish colleague. Frank Clough (*The Sun*):

Leeds paraded all the flair, drive, purpose and determination you expect to see from potential champions to slaughter title rivals Derby and, at the height of the massacre, Derby looked about as tatty and moth-eaten as turkey remains when the dog has done with it. There wasn't a single weakness as their skilled, relentless yet highly attractive football tore Derby apart.

On New Year's Day, Leeds travelled to Anfield. It proved to be the turning point of the season, and not just because of a 2-0 victory that inflicted the first home defeat in thirty-five matches on their great rivals. It summed-up the improvement in the side's performances. Don Revie said:

'It has always been an ambition of Leeds United to come here to Anfield, play well and win well. Liverpool must be the hardest team to beat at home in the world.'

Billy Bremner added:

'I was not surprised by our victory at Liverpool, as most people seem to have been. For some weeks now I have been saying how well and confidently we have been playing and how I consider we have a great chance of winning the title. It was no idle boast. I have a feeling it will be our year and recent form a results have suggested that I could well be right. We have beaten the best of the current challengers and now it is up to us to press home our claims. We have the skill and we have the confidence to do it.'

Barry Foster (*Yorkshire Post*):

Leeds United are playing their most accomplished football since they became a major power in the game. With Clarke and Jones in goalscoring mood Leeds will take some stopping. Seldom has a team started the New Year so right on the field.

Alan Thompson (*Daily Express*):

Leeds won magnificently. They have everything – ability, craft, flair, the ruthless streak, organisation and planning... Frankly they didn't have a weakness and their strengths are incalculable when measured one against the other.

Norman Wynne (*The People*):

If ever a team wore the mantle of champions elect, it was this superbly efficient outfit. The manner in which this side, who have dominated English football for so long achieved this distinction, was a convincing message to those who doubt their right to the title.

In his weekly *Goal* column Jimmy Hill noted:

A few months ago (October 1971) I wrote that I thought the League title would go to Manchester this year with City, although outsiders, slightly the better prospects. I predicted that those teams would be followed home by Derby and Liverpool so I had written off Sheffield United, who are still holding on gamely, Arsenal, Tottenham Hotspur, Chelsea and also Leeds. I seem to be pretty well on target too, apart from Don Revie and his extraordinary team. When I wrote them off it was because they were crippled by injuries and at times even a loyal fan could have been excused mistaking their team for the reserve side. Their recovery has been magnificent. If they were to win the Championship, coming from behind, it could hardly be begrudged in view of their expectations over the last couple of seasons. Leeds' 2-0 win at Anfield must have started a few knees knocking among the bookmakers.

3

Up for the Cup

Don Revie's boys embarked on the second half of the campaign at the beginning of January with a 2-2 draw against Ipswich Town. Though they failed to claim both points that would have sent them top of the table, Leeds could not be that disappointed as they had come back from being two goals down, courtesy of goals from Bremner and Clarke. Tom Holley (*The People*):

Hollywood in all its glory never staged a thriller like this... If Revie's men had to be content with a draw they at least proved they are the stuff of which champions are made by pulling themselves from the brink of defeat by sheer hard work and endeavour.

Tottenham Hotspur legend turned respected journalist Danny Blanchflower explained in his weekly column why he hoped Leeds United would come up trumps

Bremner heads home against Ipswich Town in a thriller.

in their bid for silverware. Penned prior to Leeds' FA Cup bid, Blanchflower is refreshingly honest in this extract.

Leeds have been the most polished and consistent team in the country for the past four or five years. Anybody with any football sense can see that. Of course, it has been our privilege to doubt their little shortcomings and exaggerate them like we do everything in the great game. We have nodded our heads wisely when they have just failed to hold aloft another trophy and pretended we knew their weaknesses. If we had, we could have told them how and helped them share a fortune. In truth, we have been as mystified as Leeds themselves. We could see them fail to finish but we could not see why. Perhaps the club itself was born without love and grew up without it. Revie had to fight all of that. He gave it care and attention and has produced a remarkable team in the circumstances, but the club had no great tradition to help him and always in the background lingered the thoughts of that improbable child. I find myself growing fonder of Leeds, perhaps it is my respect for Revie himself that is growing fonder. He has not got the rewards he has deserved and so fair play demands a compensation in my feelings towards him. I can see the need for his team to win something this year if Don is to maintain and advance his position… There is a law of averages that is in Leeds favour. They have had a lot of injuries to the likes of Eddie Gray, Mick Jones and Allan Clarke. They can believe that things ought to get better in that way. At full strength they will have the backing of most football judges in the country. After a slow start they are now in the forefront of the championship race and one has to fancy their FA Cup chances too because they have no other competitions in which to scatter their energies. Somehow, I have less doubts about them with regard to a winning finish this time. I know they deserve to win the league or the cup to justify their performance over the years and because I believe that, I think it will happen. Perhaps others believe it too, there will be more of us willing them on this time, and that cannot harm them. But it will be more to the point if they believe it themselves… If Leeds believe more than ever that they deserve to do it then they have a better chance. I hope they make it for Don's sake.

In the melting pot for the championship, Leeds' players turned their attentions to the FA Cup. Could the centenary year of the world's most famous knockout tournament at last be their year? Paul Reaney:

'For me the competition has always been special. There was no comparison playing an FA Cup tie to a League Cup or European tie. Everyone wants to win the FA Cup, supporters and players alike. The atmosphere in the ground was also different; it is just a magical competition. The Fairs Cup was a very hard tournament, with the top five in each country involved, the League Cup not as much, but the FA Cup with all its history was special. Despite the disappointments of previous campaigns, I knew we would win the cup eventually. It was never a sense that we would not win the cup, it was just a question of when.'

Peter Lorimer:

'There is something about the competition. Even though you may lose a final, it's a special day. You have the build-up, the occasion, the preparation, the excitement in the city. Yes, it's

Nº 05480

LEEDS UNITED
A.F.C.
TOKEN

BRISTOL R.
19
1971-72

Official Programme 5p

LEEDS UNITED
versus BRISTOL ROVERS

F.A. Cup — Third Round

Saturday, 15th January, 1972   Kick-off 3 p.m.   at ELLAND ROAD

Billy Bremner's diving header pulls one back for Leeds against Ipswich after being two down.   Photo : JACK HICKES, Leeds

Leeds United
Colours :
WHITE SHIRTS, WHITE SHORTS

1. GARY SPRAKE
2. PAUL MADELEY
3. TERRY COOPER
4. BILLY BREMNER
5. JACK CHARLTON
6. NORMAN HUNTER
7. PETER LORIMER
8. ALLAN CLARKE
9. MICK JONES
10. JOHNNY GILES
11. EDDIE GRAY

Sub........

Bristol Rovers
Colours :
BLUE SHIRTS, WHITE SHORTS

1. DICK SHEPPARD
2. PHIL ROBERTS
3. LINDSAY PARSONS
4. FRANK PRINCE
5. STUART TAYLOR
6. BRIAN GODFREY
7. KEN STEPHENS
8. WAYNE JONES
9. BOBBIE JONES
10. BRUCE BANNISTER
11. PETER HIGGINS

Sub........

Referee : Mr. A. E. MORRISSEY, Bramall, Cheshire
Linesmen : Mr. R. PORTHOUSE, Carnforth, Lancs. (Red Flag)
Mr. R. CROYSDALE, Newcastle-upon-Tyne (Yellow Flag)

WEST STAND
F.A. CUP THIRD ROUND

LEEDS UNITED
versus
BRISTOL ROVERS

ELLAND ROAD, LEEDS
Sat., 15th January, 1972
Kick-off 3.0 p.m.
RESERVED SEAT
Admit through Turnstile as allocated
ROW   SEAT No.

ADMISSION £1.00 (20/-)
Holder to retain this portion for
inspection if necessary

disappointing to lose but fans always remember because they were at Wembley when their team played. Even though you faced smaller clubs, the support would be amazing. If you played a non-league side pre-season there would be a poor attendance but if the clash was in the FA Cup the ground would be packed to the rafters. That was the magic of the competition, the small side coming to play the giants. Coaches would come from little outback places. It was their big day and would be built up by the media. Facing lower opposition was always difficult as it was like a final; there were no easy games.'

Going into the cup run Leeds sat in third spot, just one point behind leaders Manchester United. The third round draw was kind to Leeds, pairing them against Third Division outfit Bristol Rovers. Bookies made Leeds 6/1 favourites but the previous season's shock defeat at Colchester United was fresh in everyone's minds and Don Revie was determined to guard against complacency. As manager, his side had finished semi-finalists and runners–up twice. This time, in the centenary year of the competition, everyone at the club was determined to land the one domestic trophy to elude them.

Revie believed that three London teams, holders Arsenal, Chelsea and Spurs, would be the greatest dangers to his side's chances of lifting the trophy. After naming his squad, the Leeds boss commented:

'If I have fifteen men available on matchday I shall be able to give plenty of last-minute thought to team selection. This is one match I am determined to win to give us a flying start on the cup trail.'

Billy Bremner added:

'Give me the little 'uns every time. That may sound strange coming from me after the way Colchester United bundled Leeds United out of the FA Cup last season, but that defeat has not caused me to change my mind on this matter. I don't go along with players who say a First Division club at home is preferable to being drawn against clubs from the Third and Fourth Divisions. You will gather, therefore, that the draw for the third round the FA Cup, which paired us at Elland Road with Third Division Bristol Rovers, had me jumping for joy. We're delighted with it, take it from me. But having said all this, let me add that we shall treat of visitors with every respect and caution after that slip against Colchester. I doubt, however, if there are many people who will not be backing us for a place in the fourth round draw. It is not very often we lose games at Elland Road these days, and although this cup match with the Rovers is still a game which has to be won, I cannot see us slipping again.'

Bristol Rovers manager Bill Dodgin said:

'We can learn a lot from the game. It will be interesting to play against them and compare the standards. We are not downhearted by the draw and look forward to the challenge. If we went to Elland Road and defended, they would murder us. We are not afraid of them; Leeds should start worrying about us. I would rather play Leeds at Elland Road than Blyth Spartans on their ground, at least you know what you are up against.'

Rovers captain Brian Godfrey added:

'There is going to be a shock on Saturday so why not at Elland Road? We look to have the toughest of the third round ties, but we have nothing to lose. Leeds has everything. We certainly don't fear them, look what happened to them last year at Colchester. We will not be expected to do anything on Saturday except provide Leeds with their first opponents on the way to Wembley.'

With Clarke, Jones and Charlton unfit, Revie moved Madeley to centre half and recalled Reaney at right-back. Bates replaced Clarke and Jordan made his FA Cup debut in Jones' absence. Gray's appearance was his first in the competition since the 1970 FA Cup final replay.

Easing their way into the tournament, Leeds cruised into the fourth round with a workmanlike display against Bristol Rovers, ending the tie as a contest with three first-half goals on the way to a 4-1 win. Star of the show was Peter Lorimer, scoring a brace and making two for Johnny Giles. Only the woodwork and goalkeeping heroics from Rovers' 'keeper Sheppard kept the score down.

Mick Bates set up the opening goal, Lorimer's blistering drive proving too hot for Sheppard. Giles applied the finishing touch from the rebound. Lorimer quickly added a second when he ran onto a deflected through ball, before rounding the 'keeper to finish clinically. When Dick Sheppard brought down the sharpshooter, Giles fired home from the spot before supplying a pinpoint cross for Lorimer to score at the second attempt in the second half. Rovers grabbed a consolation goal shortly after the break. Keith Macklin (*The People*):

On this day of inevitable shocks and surprises it was left to the icily professional cup favourites to emphasise the necessary difference between consummate class and brave endeavour. Leeds had the game comfortably battened down in just over half an hour. From that point onwards the debate was whether Leeds would run riot, or Rovers fight back and emerge with some self-respect and pride.

During the post-match interviews, Bristol Rovers manager Bill Dodgin commented that taking on Leeds United at Elland Road with a 4-2-4 formation was slightly ambitious. Don Revie was to the point in his assessment of the match:

'This was a sound performance considering we were without Charlton, Clarke and Jones.'

Billy Bremner noted:

'I believe Rovers made a mistake in playing the way they did in their 4-1 defeat. Dodgin had said all along that his side what not play for a draw. They would come to us and they did. But I reckon their 4-2-4 tactics against a side like United was suicidal. Rovers never seemed to mark either myself or Johnny Giles tightly, with the result that were able to move about quite freely as jolly illustrated when he was on hand to slot into first goal.'

Rovers skipper Brian Godfrey said:

'If they get the luck of the draw they'll take some beating. Who wants to play at Elland Road except some non-league clubs who want some money?'

Johnny Giles recalls:

'They never stretched us at all. I scored the first when the goalkeeper failed to hold Peter's shot, my penalty made it three. Peter wrapped up the game with a brace.'

Still going strong in the centre of Leeds United's defence was Jack Charlton. Discussing his longevity with another experienced campaigner, Crystal Palace's John McCormick, Big Jack, in a *Shoot!* article called 'You Can't Keep These Veteran Stoppers Down!', noted:

'One of my stay-fit secrets is that, apart from all the training I do with the club, I give myself extra stretching exercises. Have done for a long time. I think these keep me free from injury. As for injuries, I've been lucky, I suppose. I've had one bad one and that was a torn ligament in my knee eight years ago. I fell over and twisted my knee, and it kept me out of the game for fourteen weeks. I do have a bit of trouble with a nerve working on a joint in my neck, but I haven't missed many games because of this.'

Giles notches his first goal.

Giles slots home a penalty past Rovers' 'keeper Irwin.

Regarding the future, he commented:

'They say its difficult to know when you're going off. I'm sure the crowd will tell me when I've had enough and I expect Don Revie will too. I might like a break from football, but I'd find it difficult to leave the game altogether. If I do stay in soccer, it won't be as a manager. I think the future for someone like me might be in taking charge of a team, but I don't see myself handling the business side of a club.'

Back to the League and Leeds defeated Sheffield United with an Allan Clarke goal but slipped up at Tottenham following a Sprake howler that enabled Martin Chivers to score the only goal of the match. No victories in four visits to London had the scribes writing off the team's title aspirations again, but the visitors' number six picked up rave reviews. Ken Jones (*Goal*):

It was once said of Norman Hunter that you could hear the click of his left foot cocking and that was a good enough reason for smartly getting out of the way. This obvious reference to the unforgiving nature of Hunter's tackling does him less justice now that he is firmly established as an outstanding defender and the man Leeds could least afford to lose. In a recent match against Spurs, he made more critical ball contacts around his own penalty area than some players make in a month, confirming Leeds rely heavily on his excellence and consistency. Had Bobby Moore not been around, there is no doubt that Hunter would have at least trebled his thirteen appearances for England. He's at his best when performing at Jack Charlton's shoulder and the veteran Leeds centre half has every reason to be grateful for his presence.

Don Revie told Jones:

'Bobby Moore has been a great player for England. He responds to the big occasion but my respect for Norman Hunter is linked with the fact that he does it every week for us. He was tremendous at Spurs. Nothing that he does surprises me because he is such a great professional, a great tackler and a magnificent reader of the game.'

On his hard-man image, Hunter commented:

'I never think during a game that I'd better not go in hard for fear of being booked. If the ball is there I'll go for it as hard as ever. If I'm starting to get a bit of praise now and then that won't make a difference. If it makes some players a little bit scared of me it makes my job easier. My job is to do two things. One is to stop goals being scored by getting the ball in the tackle. I want to be among them, let them know what I'm about. When I get the ball, the first part of my job is done; all I have to do is give it accurately for someone else to get on with it.'

There was not long for Leeds to dwell on travelling woes down south, as a major cup battle approached.

4

Battle of the Giants

There was an audible pause for breath from officials during the FA Cup fourth round draw radio coverage when Leeds United drew arch-rivals Liverpool at Anfield. Clearly the tie of the round, the pairing would be the first meeting in the competition between the two leading English sides since the 1965 final. Allan Clarke recalls:

'The draw traditionally took place on Monday lunchtime. After our training session we brought a radio into the dressing room and listened in. When I heard the draw, my initial feelings were of disappointment, because there was no more difficult tie than Liverpool at Anfield; however, it didn't take long to relish the challenge. We were the strongest clubs in England so it would be one hell of a game, the tie of the round. We all enjoyed playing at Anfield because the atmosphere was tremendous.'

Somewhat surprisingly Liverpool did not declare the match all-ticket, to visiting supporters' frustration. Local press noted a comment from Liverpool club secretary Peter Robinson that if fans arrived early enough they would be guaranteed a ticket. Leeds' confidence was high having won at Anfield on New Year's Day, but Bill Shankly, looking ahead to the tie, was defiant when interviewed for *Goal* magazine:

'We played them off the park until they got their first goal after sixty minutes. We were unlucky. You can't call Leeds an attacking team, they keep possession of the ball well and their passing is very accurate but they play like the continentals, negatively. In that match at Anfield the one man who gave us trouble was Eddie Gray. He was taking men on and beating them. Yet they took him off and replaced him with Mick Bates, who is more defensive.'

His side came into the match following a 4–1 victory against Crystal Palace. Shankly commented:

'It was just the tonic we needed. We have not been downhearted by our recent failure to score but our four goals against Palace will act as a tremendous fillip. If we do manage to beat Leeds I think we shall be poised to make a big impression in this year's competition. It is not often one team beats another three times in season, and I think that at Anfield it will be our turn.'

Don Revie noted the respect between the two clubs:

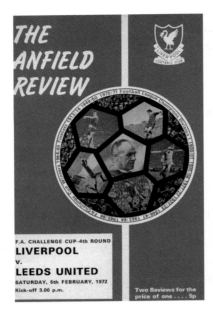

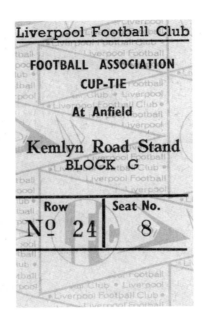

'It developed because our thinking has been along the same lines; tremendous team spirit and method. We have never been far apart in the recent past in our efforts to win League, FA Cup and European titles. We are full of confidence. I just hope the match is like the others we have played against Liverpool over the last seven years. They have been tremendous competitions, with usually just one goal in them.'

Billy Bremner said:

'There can be few more daunting tasks than facing Liverpool in the fourth round of the FA Cup at Anfield. Yet I see no reason at all why we should not go their full of confidence about the outcome. It won't be easy but then very few games are. Liverpool will be smarting after them the way we beat them in the league a few weeks ago, and this will probably make them try that little bit harder to turn the tables on us. But I'm confident we can get a good result. It will be close with very likely one goal in it, and if we do not manage to win at Anfield but I fancy our chances for bringing back to Elland Road.'

Liverpool captain Tommy Smith said:

'Games against Leeds are always tough but we always feel that if anybody is going to get a lot of goals in these matches it is us.'

Allan Clarke was relishing coming up against the Liverpool skipper.

'We had some fierce battles. Tommy was a hard player. He was a talker, continually trying to put me off my game but he never got to me and didn't stop me scoring a few goals against him over the years.'

Headlined 'The Clash of the Cup Giants' in *Goal* magazine, Ray Bradley pinpointed Leeds' top scorer Peter Lorimer as the dangerman Liverpool must watch. Don Revie told Bradley:

'Peter has had his best season since he has been at the club. He's been our key man up front. With Clarke, Jones and Gray missing through injury, Peter's vital goals have kept us up there with the leaders. Let's be frank, this boy has done a terrific job for us. He's a tremendous finisher, the hardest shot in the First Division.'

Lorimer told the reporter:

'A few seasons ago I used to be a bit of a worrier, now I just go out on the park to play. I'm not so concerned with making mistakes. I just have a go. Since then everything seems to have clicked. I'm still there to supply a few crosses but I've been getting into more dangerous striking positions. As soon as I see a chance to get into the box I take it. The boss has encouraged me to do this because I tended to stay a bit wide. Now I try to get in the box more where there are more chances to score. The goals have come and as a result I think I'm a more confident striker. I feel confident that we can win the title. For the past few seasons, we have been involved in everything. Now we've only got the league and the cup on our plate and some of the boys are beginning to complain they're not getting enough games!'

Liverpool named an unchanged team while Paul Madeley again deputised for Charlton. Eddie Gray, however, missed out, Mick Bates replacing him. In a titanic battle, Leeds' defence reigned supreme in a cauldron of noise that engulfed Anfield. Liverpool dominated possession and five times created chances, but all were wasted, the chief culprits being Steve Heighway and John Toshack. In the end, eight years of playing in pressure-cooker atmospheres throughout Europe earned Leeds a second chance. With Ian Ross man-marking Giles, Leeds failed to have the run of midfield that they experienced in their memorable win on New Year's Day. Instead their defence, led by the indomitable Norman Hunter, claimed the spoils and accolades. Norman Wynne (*The People*):

All the drama and pathos that so quickly covers the trail to Wembley were on show in this titanic clash of heavyweights that now needs a second showing. Now all eleven sweat-stained and battle-scarred heroes of Liverpool know that great heart and indomitable courage are not enough to reach the final, not if you have to beat Leeds on the way. Now the odds must surely swing heavily in Leeds' favour.

Eric Todd (*The Guardian*):

Since the competition was inaugurated 100 years ago there have been many games that the populace are pleased to call 'typical cup ties', but they never can explain what is meant by 'typical. If it may be interpreted as meaning skill, hard tackling, near-misses, over-eagerness, carelessness and refusal to surrender, then Anfield's 53,000 witnessed such a game.

Brian James (*Sunday Times*):

The shrugging shoulders of Liverpool players at the final whistle was a silent declaration of what we all know, that having proved impossible to beat, Leeds will now be the harder to hold. At full throttle from start to finish, they lacked only the precision among their forwards for the crucial thrust. Hunter and Madeley were in such form in Leeds' defence that mere passion would not do.

Commenting on Heighway's miss, Shankly said:

'It was a very good chance that we should have scored. He took his eye off the ball. You need luck to win cup matches and it was against us today.'

Johnny Giles added:

'Heighway's miss was their best chance. A cross came in from the right-hand side and he took it on his left, luckily for us he blasted it over when he should have scored. We got away with it.'

Due to an ongoing industrial dispute, the Football Association broke with a long-standing tradition by holding the fifth round draw within two hours of the fourth

Clarke checks how Bremner is after a heavy challenge.

Lorimer tries to get Leeds on the attack at Anfield.

Calm it down boys!
Referee Hill lectures
Jones and Lloyd.

No 14690

LEEDS UNITED A.F.C. TOKEN

LIVERPOOL
21
1971-72

Official Programme 5p

LEEDS UNITED
versus LIVERPOOL

F.A. CUP 4th ROUND RE-PLAY

Wednesday 9th February, 1972   Kick-off 2.30 p.m.   at ELLAND ROAD

LIVERPOOL

Leeds United

Colours :
WHITE SHIRTS, WHITE SHORTS

1. GARY SPRAKE
2. PAUL REANEY
3. TERRY COOPER
4. BILLY BREMNER
5. PAUL MADELEY
6. NORMAN HUNTER
7. PETER LORIMER
8. ALLAN CLARKE
9. MICK JONES
10. JOHNNY GILES
11. MICK BATES

Sub................................

Liverpool

Colours :
RED SHIRTS, RED SHORTS

1. RAY CLEMENCE
2. CHRIS LAWLER
3. ALEC LINDSAY
4. TOMMY SMITH
5. LARRY LLOYD
6. EMLYN HUGHES
7. KEVIN KEEGAN
8. IAN ROSS
9. STEVE HEIGHWAY
10. JOHN TOSHACK
11. IAN CALLAGHAN

Sub................................

Referee : Mr. G. W. HILL, Leicestershire
Linesmen : Mr. R. G. BOYLES, Derby (Red Flag)
          Mr. G. COOKE, Gainsborough (Yellow Flag)

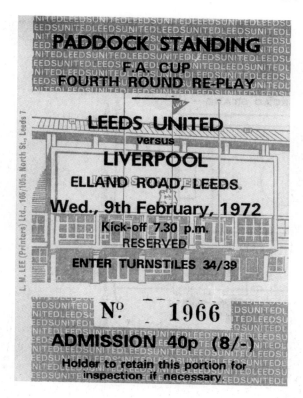

round games to help pools companies with printing deadlines. They also announced that replays would take place during daylight. The winners of the Leeds and Liverpool tie would travel to either Cardiff City or Sunderland. Regarding the draw, an FA spokesperson said:

'This is not a permanent switch, although it will take place on Saturday evening as long as the power cuts last.'

Leeds United club secretary Keith Archer commented:

'The electricity board cannot guarantee us lighting for a night match, so on safety grounds we have no alternative but to make it a 2.30 p.m. start. We were a bit disappointed on Sunday with sales but considering when the game starts the response has been overwhelming, we have been pleasantly surprised. Everything is now set for a sell-out.'

Looking ahead, FA officials announced that the centenary of the competition would be marked by a pageant before kick-off at Wembley. They would also host a banquet on the eve of the final and produce a bumper programme.

Don Revie had injury problems with Cooper, Charlton, Bremner and Gray facing fitness tests. He said:

Clarke scores a beauty against Liverpool.

'I will not name my team until thirty minutes before kick-off and I shall not be naming a squad either. I will select from my entire first-team pool. If the game is like Saturday's then all those coming will be in for a treat. We were delighted with the way our supporters rallied round this week. It cannot have been easy for them having to take the time to come down for a ticket and having to arrange time off to get to the match. I think one goal will decide it either way.'

On the day Charlton returned, Madeley replaced Bremner in midfield who partnered Clarke in attack with Jones a last-minute casualty to flu. By kick-off 10,000 supporters were locked out as an all-ticket crowd settled down for a classic encounter. In a bid to see the game a number managed to scramble onto the roof of a stand and a local pub. Others clambered up a local tree, such was their desperation to view the action, and who could blame them despite the dangers. Although injured during the early stages of the season, Allan Clarke went into the game under pressure to improve his goal output having scored only five, a paltry number by his standards.

Class always come to the fore though and Sniffer delivered when it mattered most with two sensational goals, the first a measured lob, the second a masterclass in finishing to knock out their fiercest rivals. Billy Bremner, at the hub of everything, made two vital moves in the build-up to the all-important opener. Feeding Giles with an incisive ball, a mid-air flick from Paul Madeley's return pass found the sharpshooter Clarke who lobbed incisively past a despairing Clemence. His second, though, was Clarke at his brilliant best. The move started deep in Leeds' half when Hunter robbed Heighway of possession on his own eighteen-yard line. Moving the ball to Giles, there was a quick exchange of passes with Madeley and Clarke was in possession on the left touchline. Nonchalantly beating Lloyd, Smith and Lawler, Leeds' number eight made the game safe with a cool finish when one-on-one with the Liverpool 'keeper. The Reds never gave up but Leeds' redoubtable defence held firm for a magnificent win. Watching journalists were impressed. Bill Mallinson (*Daily Mail*):

Allan Clarke answered the Leeds fans who say he does not score in important matches by settling this mini-Wembley FA Cup fourth round replay. Even Bill Shankly confessed Liverpool were beaten by 'two clever goals'. Clarke looked far more like one of the traditional Don Revie brood of home-reared internationals.

Alan Thompson (*Daily Express*):

It was the type of match between two titanic sides who could have thrilled the crowd for hours. Allan Clarke snuffed out Liverpool's FA Cup hopes with a couple of goals that only the likes of he would have the audacity to attempt.

Barry Foster (*Yorkshire Post*):

The lucky 45,821 all-ticket spectators inside the ground and some of the estimated 10,000 people outside who climbed onto hoarding and rooftops outside saw a cup tie classic. They also saw Leeds at their assured best, so much superior to Liverpool that it was hard to appreciate that Liverpool are themselves one of the most powerful sides in the country. Liverpool have now gone six full matches and 627 playing minutes without scoring against Leeds.

Don Warters (*Evening Post*):

'United's display against Liverpool had everything a successful cup side should have - plenty of drive and determination, solidity in defence, creative ability in midfield and deadly finishing.'

Referee Gordon Hill commented:

'This is the first time in my career I have applauded players off the field but it was my way of saying thank you for two of the greatest games a referee could wish to control. Both in the replay and at Liverpool these teams played like real professionals in the truest sense of the word.'

Don Revie said:

'It was a great match; we could never afford to relax against them. Clarke was at his goal-scoring best, he has been playing well for weeks and his work rate has been tremendous all season.'

Bill Shankly added:

'We were beaten by two really clever goals and we can't complain at that. When it was 1-0 I thought we had a chance.'

Billy Bremner said:

'After beating our old friends and rivals Liverpool it really doesn't matter to us who we meet in the next round. We are in the mood for practically anybody at present. It was a wonderful feeling to see the back of Bill Shankly's men, Liverpool are always a difficult side to beat, I thought we fully deserved our victory. They were two great goals from Allan Clarke but I must confess that when I flicked the ball over, to create the first chance for him I did not know whether he or anyone often a matter was there. I knew there was a strong possibility that someone would be there and in any case, those kind of balls are dangerous to any defence, as Sniffer proved. He took the goal well as he did his second.

Allan Clarke commented:

'This was my answer to the critics who say that I don't work hard enough. The boss has been on at me to get more involved and I enjoyed it this way. Quite honestly, I would have been just as happy with the result today if it had been someone else who had scored. But that's the way we think at Leeds, the result is the most important thing and it makes no difference who scores just as long as someone does. I am happy because we beat Liverpool today.'

Clarke's brace are among his most memorable strikes. He recalls:

'There was an incredible atmosphere in the ground and nothing between us, it could have gone either way. Billy then played a great ball in, I just managed to get it first and put it past the boy Clemence. My second goal gave me a lot of pleasure. I picked the ball up just inside Liverpool's half and moved forward leaving Smith on his backside. The next player that came at me was Lloyd, I dropped a shoulder and went past him. Now I was approaching the edge of the penalty area. I went past Lawler and faced Clemence who tried to narrow the angle. I ran in from the inside left position. Realising that he would expect me to curl it in at the far post I elected to go for the near one instead. Clemence gave me no more than a yard at his near post, but I hit the ball sweetly and squeezed the ball past him. That put us 2-0 up and in control. As an individual goal it was one of the best I scored.'

5

Awesome Football

Safely negotiating the opening rounds of the FA Cup, Don Revie's players were now firing on all cylinders and the coming weeks would produce some of the most memorable football played by his charges, in particular scintillating displays against Manchester United and Southampton. Sprake, Madeley, Bremner, Charlton, Hunter, Lorimer, Clarke, Jones, Giles and Gray played in both games, Cooper faced Manchester United but was injured for the Southampton clash, and Reaney deputised. Both featured on BBC's *Match of the Day*. The 5-1 victory against Manchester United brought Mick Jones his third hat-trick for the club with goals on forty-seven, fifty-eight and sixty-four minutes. His first goal was a result of following up an Eddie Gray shot and knocking in the rebound, the second came from a fine cross from skipper

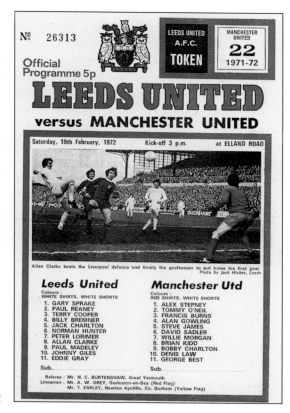

It doesn't get much better... 5-1!

Jones notches his first goal against the Red Devils.

Billy Bremner and his hat-trick goal resulted when he diverted a Peter Lorimer shot home. The result won rave reviews. Brian Glanville (*Sunday Times*):

The spectacle was almost that of the matador toying with a weary bull, the delighted roars of the crowd at each new piece of virtuosity the equivalent of the 'olés' of the bullring.

Ronald Crowther (*Daily Mail*):

Leeds, as we saw in this superb display of selfless, non-stop running, are essentially a team without any exhibitionist or would-be virtuoso. They had eleven stars all clinically efficient in this demolition of their arch-rivals from Manchester.

Tom Holley (*Yorkshire Evening Post*):

Rampant Leeds completed their 'double double' over the Manchester clubs, and if you think the Old Trafford men were 'tanned' you are dead right. It should have been 10-1. Hero of a scintillating display was Elland Road striker Mick Jones. He signalled his return after flu with a brilliant hat-trick, but he would be the first to admit the magnificent help he received from his colleagues. Gray was superb. His magnificent control and his brilliant runs had the Manchester defence at panic stations, but Revie's men were all magnificent. There was not a single position in which the Lancashire side could hold their own.

Tony Pawson (*The Observer*):

In a second half of ceaseless excitement, Leeds annihilated Manchester United, reducing their defence to fumbling incompetence. Gray sent Leeds surging into attack as he went gliding past the scything legs with elegant assurance. This was a day in which his supreme skills made Georgie very second best, giving no hint that he could match Gray's close and clever control.

Mick scores his second against Manchester United.

Take that!... Mick grabs his third.

Alan Thompson (*Daily Express*):

This was soccer sorcery and very near perfection. For twenty minutes or so Leeds produced some of the finest football sustained over a long spell that I have ever seen from any club side. Manchester at that moment looked like little children on the beach who have lost their ball to bullies and can't get it back. They never had a look at it! Few defences could have survived the sheer flowing artistry and ceaseless energy that blossomed forth from Leeds in the second half. This was a display from a team of all-stars.

Eric Todd (*The Guardian*):

Yorkshiremen are not noted for their modesty or compassion, at least in the world of sport, but on Saturday there were few who did not feel a little sad as they watched the tattered and dispirited remnants of a side which not so long ago was as proficient, eager and remorseless as Leeds are these days. The return to form of Gray was a further blow to Manchester, and after

Nice one Jonah!

scoring five, Leeds were merely bored, and Manchester chased and chased with the hopelessness of a five-year-old in pursuit of a butterfly. Sheer cruelty no less.

Mick Jones commented:

'I can't recall when we've played better, everything went right and chances just seemed to drop at my feet. Although I've missed a lot of matches this season because of injury, my job is to score, but my role involves more than that. I'm expected to stir things up, score if the chances come, but firstly create things for other players. Supporters sometimes lose sight of this, but players, especially Allan Clarke, never do, and the boss appreciates what I do and that's what matters most.'

Billy Bremner recalled:

'This was one of our best-ever performances. Since promotion our desire had been to emulate Busby's Manchester United, and this result emphasised how far we'd come. We played some fantastic stuff that day.'

Leeds' display in a 7–0 win against Southampton made *Match of the Day* viewers gasp, especially a sustained game of keep-ball when the match was comprehensively won, as much as the quality of football.

Goal 1: 39 mins: Roger Fry turns Allan Clarke's low cross into his own net.
Goal 2: 42 mins: Peter Lorimer, freed by Eddie Gray, easily beats Saints 'keeper Eric Martin.
Goal 3: 60 mins: Clarke snaps up a Giles pass to stroke the ball wide of Martin.
Goal 4: 64 mins: Lorimer's fierce strike appears to be deflected home by Bob McCarthy.
Goal 5: 70 mins: Saints are slow to clear and Lorimer provides clinical finish for his hat-trick.
Goal 6: 73 mins: Jack Charlton heads home following a cross from Norman Hunter.
Goal 7: 76 mins: Mick Jones prods home from Lorimer's headed pass from Gray cross.

An ecstatic Don Revie told reporters:

'What is there to say that can add to the performance of the lads today? The football spoke volumes for itself. Compassion it might have been, contempt it certainly was not. Theirs is the glory. They have said it all for me. I'm not saying anything. I've said it all before. You say it'.

They did. Michael Worth (*Sunday Express*):

Remember the scoreline! It marked the day Leeds United unveiled a treasure trove of memorable football riches, which they dangled temptingly before the poverty stricken beggars of

Nº 19256

Official
Programme 5p

LEEDS UNITED
versus SOUTHAMPTON

Saturday, 4th March, 1972   Kick-off 3 p.m.   at ELLAND ROAD

Photo by Jack Hickes, Leeds

Leeds United

Colours :
WHITE SHIRTS, WHITE SHORTS

1. GARY SPRAKE
2. PAUL MADELEY
3. TERRY COOPER
4. BILLY BREMNER
5. JACK CHARLTON
6. NORMAN HUNTER
7. PETER LORIMER
8. ALLAN CLARKE
9. MICK JONES
10. JOHNNY GILES
11. EDDIE GRAY

Sub.......................

Southampton

Colours :
RED & WHITE SHIRTS, BLACK SHORTS

1. ERIC MARTIN
2. BOB McCARTHY
3. ROGER FRY
4. JIM STEELE
5. JIMMY GABRIEL
6. TONY BYRNE
7. TERRY PAINE
8. MIKE CHANNON
9. RON DAVIES
10. GERRY O'BRIEN
11. BOBBY STOKES

Sub.......................

Referee : Mr. D. CORBETT, Wolverhampton
Linesmen : Mr. A. GORTON, Macclesfield (Red Flag)
Mr. P. BIRCHALL, Bolton (Yellow Flag)

Southampton. If it all seemed too easy, it was only because superb Leeds made it look that way. Southampton belonged to another league, Leeds to another world.

Noel Wild *(Sunday Mirror)*:

This was surely Leeds United's finest hour. Magical, magnificent, majestic, savage, sophisticated, surgical, brilliant, breathtaking, bemusing. You name the adjective and Don Revie's team lived up to it in the fullest sense. On this evidence Leeds are no longer just a team of great professionals. They are a team of great footballers, bursting with finesse and talent, which has blossomed over the years under Revie's guiding hand until the understanding between one player and another is now almost telepathic.

Mike Casey *(Yorkshire Evening Post)*:

Skill, individual flair, teamwork, non-stop effort and devastating marksmanship. Don Revie's Championship claimants had all these virtues in abundance.

Tom Holley *(The People)*:

Super Leeds! That was the almost ecstatic chant of Elland Road fans as rampant United brought their tally to a dozen goals in their last two games. No one can deny that they deserve the title after yet another superlative display in which they sank Southampton without trace.

Lorimer fires home against the Saints.

Big Jack heads home number six against Southampton.

Michael Carey:

Southampton was reduced to a cheap replica of a First Division side by a display of sustained, often breathtaking brilliance. Slaughter of the not-so-innocents, one might say. If it had been a boxing match or a horse race there would have been a stewards' inquiry into Southampton's limp performance. Many a towel had been thrown in before the end.

Southampton stars were quick to praise their tormentors. Eric Martin:

'I thought we were doing well until the last five minutes of the first half but then there was nothing we could do.'

Jimmy Gabriel:

'Leeds just about reached perfection. They are the nearest thing to footballing utopia. They used to be hard, niggling and unpopular, but they've come through all the phases and developed into a truly wonderful side. They're telepathic. You don't hear their players shout, they seem to know just where there mates are. Leeds have now reached the stage where they could destroy any side.'

Terry Paine:

'This was the finest performance I've seen by any team. Leeds are without doubt the finest side in the country. They did us a favour by keeping it down to seven because they were tremendous.'

Manager Ted Bates:

'When you see a team play like they did you must rate them as one of the finest in the world.'

Mick scores number seven in the annihilation of Southampton.

The match is one that Leeds players have never forgotten. Johnny Giles:

'That was a day when everything went right for us. It was a supreme performance because we played well, punished errors and got the goals. We also entertained the fans, and in my book we couldn't have done anything more.'

Mick Jones:

'When we were seven up the lads in midfield were knocking the ball about. The style of the performance was superb. People often think that it's only the midfielders who have the tricks and skills, but during the latter stages of the game all the players joined in to knock the ball about. I was stood at the front and Big Jack was at the back, we were both dreading the ball coming towards us in case we lost it! The crowd loved it, they were chanting 'olé... olé'; it was exhibition stuff and fabulous to be part of. It may have looked easy but it wasn't. It takes a lot of skill, belief and confidence to perform like that.'

Paul Reaney:

'Southampton was an easy game, we took control early on when the first goal went in, as sometimes happens in games. We did not go out to do what we did at the end of the match, it

just happened. We did not intend to take the mickey but we were so much in control we could do anything and it ended up seven.'

Paul Madeley:

'We began playing keep-ball. I remember Allan, Billy and Johnny flicking the ball about, someone had to lose the ball, which happened to be me, but I quickly won it back because I knew the stick I'd get after if I didn't. We played some magnificent football and scored some great goals, although at times it was a shade cavalier. I had to cover all over the pitch with everybody wanting to get in on the scoring. It was just incredible. I'd never known a performance like it.'

Allan Clarke:

'Our performance was as near perfection that you could get. Everything that is good about football you saw that day. There were great goals, tremendous saves, wonderful pieces of individual skill; you name it, that ninety minutes of football had it. Our sixth goal summed up our performance, because it was made by brilliant left-wing play from Norman, whose cross Big Jack headed in at the far post. Our two centre halves combining to score. Of course we played well, ask Leeds players whether the game flew; they'll tell you it did. Ask Southampton players, they'll tell you it was like eternity and wanted the game to end.'

Historically, this campaign is the only one when league doubles were recorded over both Manchester United and Liverpool. In fact, it is only the second occasion a league double had been recorded against either side in the club's history. The team rightly received national acclaim. Don Revie told reporter John Sadler:

'When we came into the First Division they slung a terrible cruel tag around our necks. They called us the dirtiest team in the land; that was a lousy label to give a team of youngsters. We were booed on every ground, booked for almost every hard tackle. It's only now that we've managed to live it down. Now they are accepting us a great team. I would like the current team to be remembered as ambassadors of football. I'm sure in years to come they will talk about us as one of the truly great football sides of world football. We are reaching the stage where we don't need to be compared to anyone. We are who we are, Leeds United. We've learned to have absolute belief in our ability. We believe in ourselves and at last other people seem to believe in us.'

Esteemed journalist Alan Hoby (*Sunday Express*) wrote:

I used to think, in their golden heyday, that Real Madrid, Manchester United, Celtic and Spurs represented poetic perfection in soccer. I used to think they were the best club sides I have seen, but I am beginning to wonder if Leeds, with their advanced tactics, their exciting elegance and flair, may outstrip all of them. For, in a soccer age dominated by highly complex football defensive systems, the ultra modern-brand of football played by the stars of Elland Road has had the critics ransacking the dictionary for superlatives. Even such fulsome phrases as the 'greatest team on earth' have been bandied around. Southampton slaughtered 7-0, Manchester United massacred 5-1, powerful Liverpool arrogantly removed from the cup, displays like these, seen by millions on TV, have stamped Don Revie's men as the side of the season. They are the team to beat.

Revie's team was at the height of its powers. Off and on the field they were a tight unit. They revelled in the banter of the dressing room and the team spirit was phenomenal but they didn't realise just how good they were. Norman Hunter:

'We knew we were a good team and had good players, but we never thought we would develop into the team that we became. We just turned up to play football, that's all you want to do, play. We were a group of lads that got on extremely well together, all you wanted to do was get up and come down to Elland Road and play. The attitude came from the individual, your personality and how your are, that can't be instilled. The lads had a will to win, and I've never been in a situation or met a group of lads where that was the most important thing. On the bus home, it mattered if we conceded a goal or lost. As a defender you always thought although you may not have been able to get close maybe you could have done something about it. We were just playing football and winning games.'

Paul Reaney:

'We didn't know how great a team we actually were. We had a sense of it and knew teams feared us by the way they talked about us on the pitch, but there again you still didn't really realise how good you are as a player or a side. Liverpool winger Peter Thompson told me once, that when he was on England duty, talk among players centred on what it was like travelling to a game at Elland Road; when they saw the Leeds sign on the outskirts of the city that was it for most teams.'

Peter Lorimer:

'Great sides have come to Leeds in the last few years and you think there is so and so, but as players you don't think that everyone thought that about you because it was just your job. We got up; we were a group of lads just doing our job. We had a great relationship with each other and it was a pleasure to do it. The thing about us was that whether we were playing a match, a game of cards, bingo, bowls or golf, everyone wanted to win. For that few minutes, it was everything to win.'

Allan Clarke:

'The players were so ambitious it was frightening. There was an amazing team spirit. Nobody knew the meaning of the word 'defeat' and our preparation was so professional. Training routines were never repetitive; everything had a purpose. Observers laughed that we relaxed by playing carpet bowls and bingo but it generated a unique team spirit. When we crossed that

white line, we died for this club. We made Elland Road a fortress. We used to watch the opposition pass our dressing room; teams were beaten before they went onto the pitch. Mike Summerbee once told me they'd just beaten Spurs by four goals. Players were chatting in the dressing room when someone asked who they had next week. Leeds was the answer, and deathly silence engulfed the room.'

Johnny Giles:

'Don developed the great drive we had as a team. He was the best around on the technical side for putting things right during a game. His attention to detail week-by-week eventually made us a great team. If I was out of position or did something wrong he'd spot it and put it right on the Monday. Many things make up a great team and it takes time to develop. There are no set of tactics a manager pulls from the sky and says we will do this today, it's about good players putting things right on an individual basis week in week out. The more faults you put right and the more matches you play, eventually you do less wrong and that is how Leeds gradually became better and better over the years. Don was superb at that. By 1968, we were beginning to become a great side. It was then a question of how long we could hold it. Great players played in a way that only great players can. The game is all about taking the right options. If somebody does this, then a great player does something else and it is impossible to stop them. That is what happened with the Leeds team. We had individually great players, a tremendous team spirit and reached an age where we had all matured. I was the second eldest. Jack was in the right position for his age, as I was for mine in the middle of the field, and so on down the team. It all gelled together. We became a great side over a period of years.'

6

Slaying the Dragons

Sandwiched between the sensational displays against Manchester United and Liverpool, Leeds returned to FA Cup action. Ten top-flight clubs remained in the fifth round draw but it took time for favourites Leeds United to find out their opponents. Eventually, Cardiff City earned the right to a plum tie following a 3–1 victory against Sunderland in a second replay. Bookies dubbed Cardiff's task 'mission impossible' with their squad totalling five caps compared to Leeds' 200-plus caps. Manager Jimmy Schoular said:

'This match has created a bigger interest here than the Real Madrid match did a year ago. My players know that it is going to be tough. It is impossible to pick out two or three danger men, they are all dangerous.'

Midfielder, Ian Gibson added:

'We all acknowledge Leeds for what they are, one of the greatest teams in the world, but our recent form shows we have no cause to be afraid on the day. We got the better of Sunderland in each of the three games against them, we have everything to gain against Leeds. They're going to get a game to remember.'

Don Revie was guarded:

'They will chase everything and fight like tigers.'

Billy Bremner commented:

'You need a bit of luck to win the FA Cup and we feel we are due some. Last year Colchester surprised us but that won't happen this time. We've played so many games before big crowds that a full Ninian Park won't bother us despite how much it will lift Cardiff.'

Revie took a fifteen-man squad on the Thursday to prepare for the 50,000 sell-out clash. Jack Charlton linked up after opening a shop in Newcastle. Media reports concentrated on the state of the Ninian Park pitch, which resembled a quagmire in areas. Twice viewing the pitch on the Friday, Revie described the surface as 'a mass of mud and water.'

Revie's assistant, Maurice Lindley said:

'In parts I sunk to a depth of three or four inches, other parts of the ground were firmer. I can't see there being much of an improvement so it looks as though it will be a difficult pitch to play on. With this sort of unpredictable surface it will not be easy to strike a true rhythm.'

Schoular added:

'I told Mr Revie that once the rain stopped the water would be gone within two hours.'

Schoular's views were soon dismissed due to continual rain resulting in the referee organising a 7 a.m. Saturday morning pitch inspection. Eventually the pitch was passed playable, although prior to and at kick-off there were two further downpours. Played on an atrocious pitch, heavily sanded, two goals from schemer Johnny Giles settled this tough-looking encounter. Leeds were in complete control throughout the tie after the Irishman grabbed his opening goal of the match, firing home a

Cardiff City A.F.C.
NINIAN PARK, CARDIFF
£1

F.A. CUP — FIFTH ROUND

CARDIFF CITY   **LEEDS UNITED**

Sat., 26th February, 1972   Kick-off 3 p.m.
ENTER THROUGH TURNSTILE 16   G. R. KEENOR, Secretary

CANTON STAND   Row   Seat No.
Block B   0   10

Giles scoring one of his goals in a comfortable 2-0 win.

rebound from a Mick Jones header. The Welsh side huffed and puffed but Giles' second, made by Allan Clarke, finished the match as a contest and signalled that it would take something very special to knock Leeds off the road to Wembley. Steve Richards (*The People*):

The trained jungle figures of Leeds mastered the Ninian Park swamp as they edged a fence nearer to the double with two masterly goals by Giles. Don Revie's skilful side not only strengthened their position as favourites, they also qualified as the meanest side in the business before an awestruck audience of 50,000. Leeds seldom gave the ball away and they revolted at the idea of anybody approaching their standards.

Jim Hill (*Sunday Express*):

The Welsh crowd watched this tie in awed acceptance at such abundant skill and talent, and were convinced that Leeds must win at Wembley. The mere presence of so much talent seemed to intimidate Cardiff. For them Jack never had a chance of being as good as his master. It made life much easier for Leeds. They were able to come to terms with the difficult pitch in their own sweet time and control the game with easy grace. They played only as well as they had to and were rarely asked to raise their game beyond a capable canter.

Don Revie commented:

'My players showed their true character and professionalism in adverse conditions today. It would have been very easy to shut up shop and play safe, but the way they have been playing recently makes that impossible. They believe they can win every game they play.'

Jimmy Schoular said:

'Leeds showed what a great side they are by being able to play on this pitch. I would back them to win the competition now.'

7

Razzamatazz

Leeds United's players almost missed the draw for the sixth round of the FA Cup on the radio as they were about to pass through a tunnel on the return journey from Cardiff when the numbers were drawn at FA headquarters, Lancaster Gate. Paul Madeley recalls:

'Two balls remained, Tottenham Hotspur and ourselves. We were delighted to get the home draw, because they were something of a bogey side to us having done the double the previous season and beaten us a few weeks before.'

Allan Clarke added:

'We knew it would be difficult, but we had been unbeaten at home for some months so we were confident.'

Controversially, Leeds United's board increased ticket prices for the clash by fifty per cent for all stand seats (£1.50) and the Spion Kop (60p, children 15p). Chairman Ald. Percy Woodward said:

'We have been very fair with the public and have done our best to make the increases hurt as little as possible.'

Tottenham were a fine side and sat only a few points behind Leeds in the league table. The Londoners had in Jennings arguably the best 'keeper around. Mike England, Phil Beal and Cyril Knowles formed a solid defence, and the Lilleywhites possessed an outstanding forward line in Martin Peters, Alan Gilzean and Martin Chivers. During the pre-match build-up, Don Revie discussed the impact of sharpshooter Peter Lorimer, identified by pundits as the man in form, with Bob Russell (*Daily Mirror*). Revie said:

'We honestly daren't let him too close to either Gary Sprake or David Harvey in case we finish up with one of our goalkeepers breaking a wrist or a finger. He's hitting the ball harder than he ever did when he won that Mirror 'Hot Shot' competition. All those hours of practice have made him quite lethal, so much so that we've had to put him out of bounds from anywhere inside the penalty area during shooting sessions. There's a new arrogance about him now, a real belief in his ability not just as an extraordinary striker of the ball but as a highly skilled all-rounder.'

№ 22393

LEEDS UNITED
A.F.C.
TOKEN

SPURS
25
1971-72

**Official
Programme 5p**

LEEDS UNITED
versus TOTTENHAM HOTSPUR

Saturday, 18th March, 1972   Kick-off 3 p.m.   at ELLAND ROAD
F.A. CUP SIXTH ROUND

LEEDS UNITED v. COVENTRY CITY—A delighted Jack Charlton turns to his team mates after
scoring on his 600th appearance for Leeds United.
Photo : JACK HICKES, Leeds

Leeds United	Tottenham
Colours :	Colours :
WHITE SHIRTS, WHITE SHORTS	WHITE SHIRTS, BLUE SHORTS
1. GARY SPRAKE	1. PAT JENNINGS
2. PAUL REANEY	2. RAY EVANS
3. PAUL MADELEY	3. CYRIL KNOWLES
4. BILLY BREMNER	4. PHILIP HOLDER
5. JACK CHARLTON	5. MIKE ENGLAND
6. NORMAN HUNTER	6. PHILIP BEAL
7. PETER LORIMER	7. ALAN GILZEAN
8. ALLAN CLARKE	8. STEVE PERRYMAN
9. MICK JONES	9. MARTIN CHIVERS
10. JOHNNY GILES	10. MARTIN PETERS
11. EDDIE GRAY	11. ROGER MORGAN
Sub..........	Sub..........

Referee : Mr. J. K. TAYLOR, Wolverhampton
Linesmen : Mr. J. B. GOGGINS, Manchester (Red Flag)
Mr. J. R. GRIFFITH, Manchester (Yellow Flag)

Lorimer, clocked at striking a ball at 75mph, was clearly enjoying his football. He told Chris Coles (*Goal*):

'I used to feel a bit underrated but now I seem to be getting my share of the headlines when I do well. I have enjoyed the extra responsibility this season and like to feel that the lads are relying on me a bit. I am always encouraged to shoot from long range, because even if I don't score, the others sometimes get goals from rebounds. Its hard to pick out my most memorable goal because I get a lot from long range but I suppose my best of the season to date was the one I scored against Manchester City at Elland Road. I didn't plan to score it that way but it dropped just right.'

Regarding the Tottenham clash, the Leeds boss told Alan Hoby (*Sunday Express*):

'We respect all our opponents but we have more respect for Spurs than most. However, we like to think that we are going back to Wembley for the third time in seven years. Nothing is certain in this game but I have never seen the boys so relaxed or enjoying their football so much. They have learned from adversity to take hard knocks and to overcome them.'

Speaking with journalists on the eve of the match, Revie said:

'This is a terrific tie, tough of course because Spurs are a world-class side, but at this stage of the competition you don't expect anything else other than a hard game. We are ready and fully prepared, everything has gone well this week and we have no injury problems. Their defence is

excellently organised and they have an effective offside trap, but I think we have worked out a way to beat it.'

Johnny Giles described the clash in *Goal* as just another game, albeit a tougher one than normal. He said:

'Spurs have a good record against us over the last two seasons, but a bogey side? We don't have any bogey teams. We respect Spurs as a very good side and they have played well against us this season. So what? A lot of good sides play well against Leeds. Spurs are a dangerous side, they must be with players like Chivers, Peters and Gilzean up front but we've got a few good forwards ourselves. In any case everything's completely different in the cup. It's a sudden death competition and the sort of challenge we've been reared on.'

Billy Bremner commented:

'The game will be a hard one but if we get the breaks early on, I believe we have the ability and skill to win by three goals. Knowing how Spurs play I should think they will play very tight at the back, relying on Chivers and Gilzean to snatch a goal. We are approaching the game confidently and I am backing us for place in the semis.'

Spurs manager Bill Nicholson was cautiously optimistic:

'You couldn't ask for a harder tie than this, but all teams are difficult once you reach this stage of the FA Cup. There's certainly no reason for depression. We shall go to Leeds and do our very best. We beat them at home in January and drew against them at Hull earlier in the season. That's an encouraging record.'

His players were bullish. Mike England said:

'Of course we were disappointed when we found out it was Leeds. Anywhere away would be tough, but this is the hardest of the lot. However, we've got a good record against them and we're pretty confident in the way we are playing at the moment, so I don't see why we shouldn't get through. A draw up there would do us nicely as I think we can beat them in a replay at home.'

Martin Chivers added:

'I can't see Leeds dictating the game against us as they do against other teams. All teams tend to be a little more cautious in a cup tie than they are in a league game, even if they are playing at home.'

John Pratt concluded:

'We never play badly against Leeds. Every team has a club they don't like playing, we are that to Leeds.'

Prior to kick-off the Football Association somewhat unusually had to rule on shirt clashes for all four ties. All were resolved – Leeds, as the home team, chose all-white. They could not have been in a better frame of mind, coming into the clash on the back of a 7-0 win against Southampton. Revie was determined to capitalise on the positive press his team was attracting and announced before the Tottenham game that his players would perform warm-up exercises before kick-off, wear tracksuit tops with names emblazed on the back and numbered stocking tags. He said:

'The fans have been absolutely tremendous this season and everyone at the club is delighted with our support. We want to show them how much we value the packed attendances and the

Clarke poaches Leeds' equaliser against Tottenham.

fact that they are right behind us. I feel that the crowd wants to associate with the players and we want them to feel part of the club. The most important people in the game are the people who pay the wages, the fans who support us and help us build and improve. We want them to share our success in the club.'

When the action finally began, Leeds displayed their attacking prowess. It should have been over by the interval as Leeds hit the bar through Allan Clarke and created countless chances, but they could do little about the inspirational form of 'keeper Pat Jennings with a string of superlative saves to deny Mick Jones, Terry Cooper and Clarke. Pat Jennings' expertise at one point looked as if it may take his side to victory after his opposite number Gary Sprake gifted the visitors a first-half lead totally against the run of play following John Pratt's speculative forty-yard cross from a free-kick, but Clarke's sharpness brought an immediate equaliser on the stroke of half-time. From then it was only a question of time for the winner to arrive and Jack Charlton obliged to send his side into the last four of the competition for the second time in three seasons. Don Revie was delighted:

'The way we knock the ball about amazes me. Against a very strong Spurs side I thought our football for twenty minutes was absolutely fantastic. The side showed character by bouncing back to win after being one down. Who needs Dixie Dean and Tommy Lawton after a goal like Charlton's? Jennings was fantastic, he made several world-class saves, especially two from

Close call!

Big Jack heads home the winner
against Tottenham.

Cooper and Jones. He must have cost us seven or eight goals today. We have played well many times this season but I reckon this was our peak. We had to pick ourselves up after Spurs had taken the lead. That showed our character and for the rest of the match I give Jennings credit for keeping the scoreline respectable.'

Bill Nicholson said:

'My players thought they could play until they saw this. Leeds were unforgettable.'

Jack Charlton commented:

'It was easy really. We were simply too good for them. My winner was quite simple. I was going to go for the near post, but changed my mind. Billy Bremner's free-kick was perfect and there was nothing really difficult about heading it in. It's unusual for me to see the ball and goal together, then be able to pick a spot, and knock it in exactly where I wanted it to go.'

Pat Jennings added:

'They might as well give Leeds the FA Cup now. I can't see any team left in the competition that could beat them on the form they have been showing over the last few weeks.'

The media was impressed with Leeds' performance. Alan Thompson (*Daily Express*):

Just stay as great as you are. You have the best gimmick known wherever the game is played, untold ability and yes, greatness. The translation of the Spanish word 'real' is 'regal, royal' and Leeds are just that in a football sense.

Brian James (*Sunday Times*):

A match that had as many moments of near perfection as football can get. Nothing in Tottenham's experience could have quite prepared them for the ordeal they faced against a fine side achieving its ultimate and certainly nothing could have armoured Spurs against the swift and deadly flow of the football that so nearly annihilated them.

Eric Todd (*The Guardian*):

On this form, Leeds are irresistible. They have some outstanding individuals, Madeley alone is worth £300,000 of anybody's money, and when those individuals put the team before self-aggrandisement and pool their assets, the result is awesome.

Hugh McIlvanney (*The Observer*):

Only bigots can now bet against them (Leeds) in the competition. This was a day when Don Revie's comparisons with the greatest of European teams could not be dismissed as ludicrous arrogance. Their football was breathtaking in its scope and fluency, alive with dazzling improvisations. The full intimidating depth of their quality has never been more manifest than it was in those early minutes. There was scarcely a weakness to be seen and excellence everywhere.

Terry Brindle (*Yorkshire Post*):

Leeds should be a short-price for the Boat Race, the Grand National and the British Grand Prix (on foot), let alone the cup!

Billy Bremner recalled:

'*That was one hell of a game, one of the greatest I ever played in because Tottenham played outstanding that day and so did we. In the end we just scraped home.*'

Paul Madeley added:

'*Allan and Big Jack pulled it round for us. Towards the end we soaked up a little bit of pressure as Spurs needed to throw everything at us, and did. Of course the occasion was heightened because it was a quarter-final clash, a packed house and two big teams were involved but the atmosphere throughout was electric, and is one of the best games I ever played in at Elland Road.*'

Regarding the razzamatazz, Madeley recalls:

'It was Don's idea for us to wear the stocking tags and warm up in front of our fans. Les Cocker impersonated a 'sergeant major' and had us all in two's hopping and skipping to loosen up. The Tottenham game was the first time that we did this and it had an incredible effect on everyone. The crowd was electric. Nowadays a warm up is the norm but in 1972 it was very different. Of course, away supporters gave us stick but our fans enjoyed it and we did it everywhere we played.'

Leeds' recent performances resulted in a cavalcade of tributes from pundits. Arguably television's top soccer expert at the time, Jimmy Hill devoted his weekly *Goal* column to praise the West Yorkshire giants. Hill wrote:

My goodness, what a magnificent side Leeds have become and I don't mean that as an insult to their performances in the past. I wouldn't name them as the club most likely to be 'Top of the Pops', but brilliant performances on television recently have enhanced their reputation immeasurably.

They eliminated Tottenham from the FA Cup competition by a score of 2-1, but that score only revealed a small part of the story. It didn't disclose one of the finest goalkeeping performances for many a long day from Irish international Pat Jennings. We have always known what a brilliant goalkeeper Pat is, but I don't think he has ever made more spectacular saves in one game of football. The score didn't take into account, either, Tottenham's relentless determination not to be beaten at Elland Road but stopping Leeds was like trying to hold back the tide. Neither could the score possibly show the sheer creativity of Leeds' footballing skill, the finest pattern of football they have produced yet.

Without any doubt such football is a culmination of many years of hard work and striving, with a fair measure of disappointment punctuating periods of success. The question is, what factors have made it come so good? I think it's the improved form of two players, Eddie Gray and Mick Jones.

There has never been any question as to Eddie's ability, but he has had lengthy periods of inactivity through injury, which has prevented him stringing a run of fluent performances together. Those injuries created doubts that he might never fulfil his destiny. Suddenly, it all seems to be there… dribbling ablity, running power, explosive finishing and cunning and, unless you are one of Eddie's opponents, it's a pleasure to witness.

What has happened to Mick Jones is more of a mystery. I have written before of his value to the Leeds team. His commitment and brave running up front to take passes from defence is a vital necessity. Maybe, as a result of this, his goalscoring record has deteriorated in recent years and there's nothing worse for a striker than not scoring goals. In modern football the striker's role is unquestionably the most difficult. Apart from all the skills and physical strength needed, it takes the confidence of a Muhammad Ali to maintain consistent form. Although Mick has always made a contribution to Leeds' success, there is now an extra edge and sharpness to his game; he looks more potent in front of goal and so much more relaxed in everything he does. This extra success is a fitting reward for the efforts of a most genuine player.

Jones scores against Forest.

The old star ingredients in the Leeds side are shining as brightly as ever. Jackie Charlton goes on agelessly; Billy Bremner and Johnny Giles are masterful and unstoppable in the middle of the field. They are football artists to their fingertips and have carved their own niche in football history as all-time greats. In their present form, Leeds look good enough to take on twelve or thirteen opponents, let alone eleven, and the fabulous football they are producing is fitting tribute to the leadership, the imagination and the resolution of Don Revie, his board and his staff. It's all very well restoring a club to its former glory, but they have taken Leeds United to a pinnacle that it has never known.

Safely through to the semi-finals, Leeds returned to the title race and their battle with league leaders Manchester City, Liverpool and Derby County. Impressive victories against Arsenal and Nottingham Forest followed a win against Coventry City, a match in which Jack Charlton marked his 600th league appearance with the only goal of the match, and a draw at Leicester City. Following the 3-0 win against the Gunners, a match in which Billy Bremner presented Arsenal skipper Frank

McLintock with a silver tankard to mark his side's double achievement the previous season, McLintock (*Goal*) said:

'*Leeds were tremendous. They are the best team in the First Division and deserved to win the title because of the way they play. We've played Derby and Manchester City, but this Leeds team is just fabulous.*'

Alan Ball added:

'*Tremendous. Defensive mistakes helped them to a couple of goals but do not let me take anything away from them. They are a truly wonderful side.*'

Don Revie, commenting on his side's first-half display that resulted in all three goals, said:

'*I've never seen them play so fast for forty-five minutes. They deserved their wonderful standing ovation from the fans. Frankly, they have been amazing for weeks and they must take all the credit. The pressure we put on Arsenal in the first half was terrific. Nobody can coach a team to play like that. It is the natural, individual flair, which makes them the team that they are.*'

Journalists eulogised. Brian Glanville (*Sunday Times*):

In a spirit more reminiscent of Christmas than Easter, Leeds United, having gone through their new Busby Berkley antics, clapped Arsenal on to the field, presented them with a silver tankard, then beat them out of sight.

Big Jack heads home on his 600th League appearance for Leeds.

Lorimer sets up another Leeds attack against the Gunners.

Nicely does it! Allan scores a goal against Arsenal in a 3-0 win.

Eric Todd (*The Guardian*):

I do not know whether Arsenal and Tottenham Hotspur are on speaking terms. If they are, Tottenham, who were on the receiving end a week ago at Leeds, must have forgotten to warn Arsenal what to expect. They, like Tottenham, must have marvelled that they escaped so lightly. Every adjective, not every one complimentary of course, has been allocated to Leeds these past few years. Most of them were relevant and justified, but few of us ever expected 'merciful' to be applicable.

Leeds' 6-1 win against Forest was clinical but had a lot to do with an injury to 'keeper Jim Barron. His three minutes on the sidelines from the fifty-fifth minute, with Peter Cormack deputising, saw the score jump from 1-1 to 3-1. From that position there was no way back for the visitors. Leeds' goal haul, thanks to braces from Lorimer, Clarke and Gray, took their tally to twenty-two in five home matches.

  With Leeds once again challenging for double as the Easter fixtures approached, Ray Bradley interviewed Johnny Giles in depth for *Goal* magazine. Summing-up fixtures at West Ham and Derby prior to a derby clash at Elland Road against West Yorkshire neighbours Huddersfield Town, Giles said:

'These Easter games are the crunch games for every top team. All the previous work centres on how we do in these vital holiday clashes. You've got to aim for a maximum of six points and we'll be hoping for at least four out of six but it all depends on how your rivals do.'

Regarding Leeds overcoming their tough start, the Leeds schemer said:

'Early on we had an unsettled side. We were without our top two strikers Allan Clarke and Mick Jones, and Eddie Gray missed nearly half the season with a shoulder injury. You take three top players like that out of any First Division side and you are bound to suffer. Peter Lorimer was our only recognised striker and his goals early on were priceless but we really started picking up the points when we were back to full strength. Looking back, it was probably our worst start to the season for years and everyone tended to write us off but they underestimated our character. We never gave up because we know the championship is a long race. In my opinion, Coventry was our worst team display for many seasons and afterwards we were all a bit disgusted with our performance. We got a lot of stick from the press and it hurt. We were determined to wipe that one out and with Jones and Clarke back for the next match we beat Manchester City 3-0, a great performance that boosted our confidence and started off a run of fourteen games in which we lost only one match. When you lose in this game it's no use crying about it. You must pick up the pieces and start all over again. We've got the character in this side to do that.'

Asked if Leeds had peaked as a team, Giles said:

'It's impossible to answer that. Certainly I think we are playing better now that at any time in my eight years at the club. When we won the championship three years ago people said we had reached our peak then, but I think we are a more confident, mature and

polished side now and on top of that we are scoring far more goals. Surely that is the best barometer.'

Do Leeds rely on individual flair and skill rather than graft and teamwork? Giles responded:

'All the time. We've been called a machine and we take that as a compliment to our teamwork, but it's the players who make the machine work. Bad players make a poor machine. Every team has an image and I suppose that's ours, but the skill and the flair are the cogs that oil the machine and make it efficient and smooth running. We've got world-class players like Bremner, Gray, Clarke and Cooper. You can't dismiss people like that as just part of a machine. People in the game respect us because we are a great side, a combination of all talents.'

Explaining his 'telepathic' understanding with Billy Bremner, Giles said:

'Basically it's purely instinctive. Obviously it has grown stronger over the years we've played together, but it's still instinctive. You can plan and devise all sorts of ploys in practice but in the end its your instinctive reaction to a set situation that counts. Every game provides a fresh challenge; you've got to think and improvise as you go along, to try to read situations. I like to try to find a bit of extra space to give myself extra time to react, and that's where Billy and I read one another perfectly.'

Discussing his 'hard man' reputation, Giles commented:

'Perhaps I'm a more competitive player since I joined Leeds, but basically my attitude to the game hasn't changed. If people want to play football then I want to play football because I've always tried to be a creative player. If someone wants to mix it, I can take care of myself. It's as simple as that.'

Following an Eddie Gray brace to salvage a 2-2 draw at West Ham, Leeds were well-beaten 2-0 in a crucial match on Derby's muddy and treacherous Baseball Ground pitch. Frank McGhee (*Sunday Mirror*):

Statistics sometimes tell a revealing story and the harsh truth is that Leeds had only one shot at the Derby goal in the whole first half, an illegal one at that. Bluntly the story of this match was the failure of too few Leeds players to perform as valiantly away from home as they do at Elland Road.

Barry Foster (*Yorkshire Post*):

Derby never allowed Leeds to settle on the ball and play the game at their pace. It is a formula that has beaten Leeds before but, one should quickly add, Derby backed up their pressure with a great depth of skill and ideas.

Derby delight – Mick scores against West Yorkshire neighbours Huddersfield Town.

Leeds bounced back with three-goal victories against Huddersfield and Stoke City. The result at the Victoria Ground was one of the most significant of the season, although it came at a heavy price when Terry Cooper broke his left leg six minutes from time after an innocuous-looking brush with Marsh, just a week before his side's FA Cup semi-final clash with Birmingham City. Leeds' star man was Mick Jones with a brace.

STOKE CITY F.C.

Saturday, April 8th 1972
Kick-off 3.15 pm

STOKE CITY
v
LEEDS UNITED

OFFICIAL PROGRAMME · 6p

8

Next Stop Wembley

The FA Cup semi-final draw paired Leeds United with Birmingham City. Don Revie commented:

'We will play where we are told to play, we do not mind playing where the Football Association decide.'

Birmingham manager Freddie Goodwin was unhappy the clash was scheduled at Sheffield Wednesday's Hillsborough ground. He said:

'We are objecting because it is much further for our supporters to travel and it gives Leeds supporters a much better chance of getting to Sheffield for extra tickets. We had Goodison Park, Maine Road or Old Trafford in mind. We are telephoning the Football Association and a letter of protest will follow.'

Allan Clarke recalled:

'Stoke City, Arsenal and ourselves wanted Birmingham. We were delighted.'

Goodwin's appeal was eventually turned down. Looking ahead to the clash he said:

'Being drawn against my old club is wonderful. If you take the two sides and analyse them closely, and take into account their experience, United come out on top, but Birmingham have been playing reasonably well this year and given a couple of breaks we could still get to Wembley. The players are in perfect trim to take on Leeds.'

As in the previous round, the Football Association had to resolve the strips for both sides. Leeds submitted three choices, all white, all yellow, and all red. After some discussion, Leeds agreed to wear all yellow, Birmingham red and white stripes. In the week of the game, Alan Hughes (*Goal*) predicted:

It should be quite an FA Cup final, Leeds and Stoke, even though it will add up to a bittersweet Wembley for broken-leg victim Terry Cooper who will watch it with anguish filling every single minute. That's a forecast that will get me banned from every boozer within a few miles of my native St Andrews, and I don't suppose Arsenal fans will care if I never show my face around Highbury again, but Leeds v. Stoke is the only final that makes sense. The danger to Leeds is only that they underestimate Second Division Birmingham, and don't tell me that Leeds have never been guilty of underestimating anybody, because there was that embarrassing confrontation with Belgium unknowns Lierse, which cost the Elland Road side their place in the UEFA Cup. Leeds are more skilful than Birmingham, have more big-match experience, have the greater method and in fact have the greater incentive because Birmingham manager Freddie Goodwin has spelled out to his players that promotion is what matters at St Andrews.

With Terry Cooper out, Paul Madeley switched to left-back enabling Paul Reaney to return at right-back, an ironic situation for Reaney who missed out on the 1970 FA Cup final due to a broken leg. Reaney recalls:

'It was a difficult time for me because I was in and out of the side. It was strange because, in 1970, I'd have played in the final and but for TC's broken leg in '72 I'm not sure if I'd have been in the side. We had such a good side and it just shows you how luck goes. I knew how TC was feeling, but that really finished him. He never really recovered. Semi-finals are not easy games to play in; there is so much tension because of what is at stake.'

For Paul Madeley, this was his fourth positional change of the cup run, which once again demonstrated his versatility. Starting the campaign at centre half due to an injury to Charlton for the opening two matches, Madeley deputised for Jones in the Liverpool replay, before switching to right-back for the fifth round and quarter-final matches. Cooper's injury meant four positional changes, one few footballers could achieve seamlessly. Madeley was used to different roles and when pundits name the great Don Revie X1, his name fails to appear. Incredibly though, the side often quoted; Sprake, Reaney, Cooper, Bremner, Charlton, Hunter, Lorimer, Clarke, Jones, Giles and Gray, only lined up once, for an FA Cup clash against Mansfield Town in 1970. Madeley says:

'It's bizarre, but I understand it because I would also name this XI. However, throughout my years at Leeds I always played and expected to play. Indeed, I'd have been disappointed if I wasn't picked.'

For Leeds United's 'Rolls Royce' the midfield anchor role was his preference. He says:

'Playing alongside Billy and Johnny in midfield was great. They were so natural as a partnership and complemented each other so well. My role was straightforward. I was the anchorman to protect the back four, and after winning the ball would serve it up to either of them. It was an easy job really, I didn't need to think about playing a through ball; I was content to give it to the masters. However, I did have licence to move through, and I exercised this whenever possible. It was wonderful to play behind them; they were both so capable on the ball. Their control and vision was amazing. They were both so aware of what they would do with the ball, before they received it. I spent a lot of my career marking out the danger man of the other side, which was very satisfying when you do it right, but not nearly as much as being

able to express yourself, which arose when the opposition concentrated their attentions on Billy or Johnny. Playing this role gave me some of my best memories as a player. Wearing all the different shirts was a bit of an illusion though because I played midfield in so many games wearing number eleven, ten, or eight depending on who was injured. I always joked about it.'

Interviewed in *Goal,* by Ray Bradley, about the clash with the midlanders, Madeley noted:

'Most of the current team are only names to me, but any side that reaches the semi-final must be good and we certainly shan't underrate them, especially at this crucial stage of the competition. Birmingham will be treated with the same respect as top First Division opponents, but accepting that, I'm still confident that we shall reach Wembley again. Semi-finals are usually scrappy affairs because so much is at stake, but our greater experience should get us through in the end. This is a game we've got to win because we want to win the FA Cup for the first time in our history. We've had our fair share of disappointments in the past, so now we must make sure. We have really clicked in the last two months and are playing better than at any time in my career with the club. The team has hit spells like this before, but I doubt if we've ever played with more collective confidence. The return of Gray, Clarke and Jones up front has really pepped us up. We are really creating a lot more chances now and this has been reflected in our overall confidence. There has been a difference in our style of play for three seasons now and I think our finishing in the last few months has been much sharper.'

Don Revie knew the value of his star utility player:

'People get agog about Paul Madeley's ability to play in different positions that they tend to forget he's a world-class player. However, you cannot exaggerate his value. Having him at the club is like having three men in one. He can do any job. Paul just goes out and does exactly what you want him to do; I never need to worry about him.'

Looking ahead to the clash, Revie said on the eve of the match:

'There's something different about an FA Cup semi-final and until you have experienced it you do not realise what it's like. On the morning of the match, the fact that you are only ninety minutes away from Wembley hits you all of a sudden; it can be a nerve-wracking feeling. The tension continues to mount as the morning goes by and hits a peak when you get to the ground. We have been at this stage five times in the past seven years and feel we are well equipped for the big occasion and its tensions. It must be an advantage to us.'

Revie's team talk brought a major surprise when David Harvey, who played superbly at Stoke in Sprake's absence through injury, was told he would keep his place in preference to a fit-again Sprake. Billy Bremner recalled:

'We were sitting in the Sheffield hotel on matchday when the gaffer told us the team. As he announced Harvey's name, I glanced over at Gary who just walked to the entrance of the hotel

ONE STEP TO WEMBLEY

Leeds United v Birmingham City

FA Cup semi-final souvenir

The glory of Leeds United's march on Wembley is crystallised in one magic moment as striker Allan Clarke drives home the equaliser in the sixth-round tie with Spurs watched by skipper Billy Bremner and helpless defender Phil Beal.

Evening Post special publication

March 1972 Price 3p

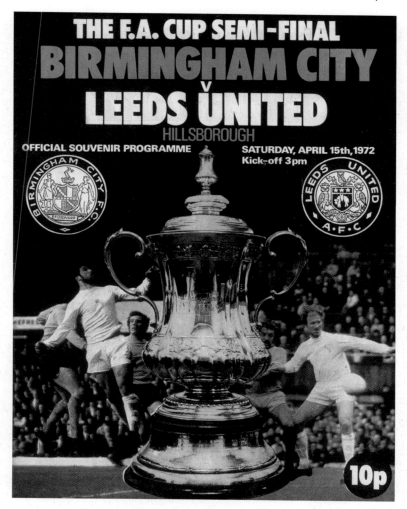

shaking his head in disbelief. I think the gaffer got a tip that Latchford was going to try unnerve Sprakie at the first opportunity. To my mind leaving an experienced goalkeeper out in favour of a young fella was a gamble for a match of this importance. David substituted Gary in a European Cup semi-final but telling a young boy he is playing in a semi-final on merit was different.'

Norman Hunter:

'We never discussed it with Don until some years after Gary left the club but David was picked and that was it. Looking back, Gary should have been dropped earlier but the gaffer was loyal. Ability-wise there was no one better but it was his concentration; he just lapsed. If Gary was under pressure during a game, he was class and had more good games than bad, but as a defender sometimes I never knew what he was going to do. He'd come and stop, whereas David was not the best at crosses but when he did come he let you know and rarely made mistakes.

When Gary was on song there was no one who could take them better, but other times he'd say mine, yours, sorry. David was calm and great to play with. He should have come in a couple of years earlier.'

Peter Lorimer:

'Although he was performing well, we knew as a group Gary's bottle had gone, you could see it and could catalogue his mistakes; Crystal Palace, when he dropped the ball for a last-minute equaliser, Everton in an FA Cup semi-final and the Chelsea final. Teams realised that if you got about Gary he'd crack. Colchester came out to ruffle him up and he just couldn't cope with it. It was no great surprise to me when it happened and should have occurred earlier.'

The Leeds boss went through his dossier detailing Birmingham's strengths and weaknesses. Allan Clarke recalls:

'The gaffer pointed out Birmingham's full-backs tended to cover too wide or push forward too much, leaving gaps behind them. Normally he would tell Peter and Eddie to get down the bylines before crossing the ball from the dead-ball line, but for this game, he told them to knock quick crosses in from the edge of Birmingham's penalty area. He told Johnny and myself to peel off to the back stick to exploit this space.'

When Leeds' players ran out up to limber up Birmingham's players attempted to imitate the Yorkshire side's somewhat infamous pre-match routine. Norman Hunter recalls:

'Freddie Goodwin tried to unsettle us by sending his team out before us to warm up. They were so disorganised it was laughable, each player chased after the person in front attempting to keep up. We went about our normal routine at one end of the ground while Birmingham embarrassed themselves in the centre-circle. Their attempt to upstage us completely backfired.'

From the outset, there was never any doubt that Leeds would win this game. The hero of the hour was Mick Jones with a brace of goals, Peter Lorimer grabbing the other. David Harvey made two smart saves, one particularly impressive from Bob Latchford. Jones' opening goal came on the back of a brilliant move involving Paul Reaney, Lorimer and Johnny Giles. His second (Leeds' third) followed a simple knock back from Clarke following a deep cross from Lorimer, who notched the second goal himself with a clinical strike after Eddie Gray had cut open Birmingham's square defence. Recalling the first goal, Clarke recalls:

'All we did was play to the gaffer's instructions at the team meeting. We were attacking down the right flank and Peter crossed the ball quickly. I peeled away because I saw the right full-back moving out and with little difficulty placed the ball across the six-yard box. Mick just ran onto it and popped it in.'

There was a great sense of satisfaction in the Leeds dressing room. Don Revie:

'Mick's goals were magnificent examples of his running power and being in the right place at the right time.'

Billy Bremner:

'David made some great saves but the game went the way I expected it to go.'

Norman Hunter:

'The semi-final was the easiest of my life. We were so much in control. Billy and Johnny were pinging it all over the place, doing what they wanted. David made a good save at 0-0, if that went in it's a different ball game but once Peter stuck the second in the bottom corner the match was over. We were so quickly on top we were rolling, and strolled it.'

David Harvey:

'I played against Stoke the previous week but I felt this was the big one, the big chance. Before, when I made occasional appearances I knew that often I was still learning the trade but this time I felt that I was capable of keeping my place.'

Jones and Hynd tussle for the ball.

'Sniffer' Clarke sets up his partner for the first goal against Birmingham City.

Knockout punch – Leeds are on their way to Wembley.

Jack Charlton:

'The wind made things difficult for us, it wasn't easy to play against it and we took a little bit longer to settle down than I would have liked. Once we scored I knew we would be all right, but still I wouldn't say it was an easy win. It was comfortable but not easy.'

Peter Lorimer:

'The greatest feeling you get is when the final whistle goes in semi-final and you have won the match. You think, that is it, that is your year, you are going to Wembley.'

Allan Clarke:

'Reaching Wembley is so important to a player. When the referee blows the whistle at the end of a semi-final and you know you're at Wembley, the feeling is fantastic. You know that on FA Cup final day you will be on television all over the world with millions watching. It's a great feeling.'

Mick Jones:

'My goals weren't the best I ever scored, one was a knock-in from four to five yards out, the other was chested in on the goal-line, but they all count. In the end it was a very comfortable victory, our big-match experience told throughout.'

Paul Madeley:

'It was over by half-time and we ran out comfortable winners. Overcoming Birmingham was great, but there was no great celebration, we wanted to finish the job. After the Chelsea defeat Don said we'd be back; he was right. My most poignant memory was Terry Cooper hobbling over towards me. Despite his own personal disappointment at missing out on Wembley he was thrilled for everybody.'

Freddie Goodwin was philosophical:

'There's no getting away from it Leeds are a great side, they deserved to win. Up to Jones's first goal I thought there was little between the sides. We had our chances but unlike Leeds did not put them away.'

Leeds' professional display was well received by pundits. James Mossop (*Sunday Express*):

Don Revie's masters turned on a show that was something special: a strolling show of style, grace and skill that brought rare moments of soccer magic. Not for Leeds the nervous, frenzied play that traditionally reduces semi-finals to scrappy, scrambling affairs.

Derek Potter (*Sunday Express*):

Birmingham spent most of the ninety minutes running round in circles desperately chasing to contain a coldly calculating Leeds, magnificently generalled by Johnny Giles. Giles can rarely have dominated a match more. Intelligent positional work meant that anyone in trouble could find Giles in space, willing to undertake responsibility and switch the line of defence or attack.

Eric Todd (*The Guardian*):

Only once on Saturday did Birmingham City take the mickey out of Leeds United, and because it happened before the game it didn't really matter. Not often does class distinction amount to much in cup football, but here was an exception. Birmingham looked what undoubtedly they are, a good Second Division side; Leeds again were formidable representatives of the First Division and at no time did the twain meet.

Don Warters (*Yorkshire Evening Post*):

The game went very much according to expectations, with Don Revie's double-chasing side in control and turning on one of their now frequent displays of powerful all-round effort and skill. There was little the Blues could do about the situation except, keep trying.

Celebration time after another goal in
the semi-final win over Birmingham.

Boys of '72

Brian James (*Sunday Times*):

A result as inevitable as tomorrow's dawn.

Mike Casey (*Yorkshire Evening Post*) analysed each player's performance:

David Harvey: *His coolness, safe-handling and determined resistance in face of City's jostling tactics, particularly by Bob Hatton, instilled confidence in his fellow defenders.*
Paul Reaney: *The England full-back, besides playing a key role in the all-important first goal, was here, there and everywhere as the Midlanders desperately flung themselves into attack.*
Paul Madeley: *The most versatile player in the country never gives anything less than a five-star performance. This match was no exception. His occasional overlapping, in a fair imitation of the injured Terry Cooper, and resolute defensive work must have broken the will of the opposition.*
Billy Bremner: *United's skipper, unruffled by the occasion, again worked well with midfield partner Johnny Giles, finding plenty of time to lend a hand with the strikers. But one sensed that he never really needed to throw himself 100 per cent into the fray, so superior were his side.*
Jack Charlton: *If the veteran international with the Peter Pan approach to the game had heard of Bob Latchford and Bob Hatton's scoring exploits, he showed no signs of it. This colossus strode through the match. What a lion-hearted player!*
Norman Hunter: *United's 'Iron Man' was always there to break up any threatening danger. His ferocious but always fair tackling was too much for the steely Birmingham players. One even shied away from a confrontation as Norman thundered into view!*
Peter Lorimer: *The talented Scot with the hottest shot in British football scored his twenty-ninth goal of the season and did much fine work besides. His splendid centre, which led to Jones' first goal would have done credit to that most accurate of kickers, Johnny Giles.*
Allan Clarke: *He never gave up foraging, chasing, looking for the chance of a quick shot. His presence spelled danger and, in marking him so closely, Birmingham left gaps, which were quickly exploited by United's other front runners.*
Mick Jones: *It was wonderful to see the energetic, fearless striker notch two goals after all his hard work this season. So often criticised for his lack of scoring power, he answered the best answer to the 'knockers'. His play off the ball caused tension in the City defence, a big factor in United's triumph.*
Johnny Giles: *The robust schemer-in-chief set up two of the goals and was a constant worry to the harassed opposition. His play was a joy to watch, his dainty avoidance of flying boots breathtaking.*
Eddie Gray: *United's answer to George Best tormented Birmingham until they hardly knew which way to turn. Superb ball control, speed and a keenness to tackle, which has not always marked his play, made him a key player in United's team.*

To sum up: *United's play was loaded with skill, vigour and imagination... cup soccer at its best.*

9

Twin Towers Here We Come

Three weeks separated the FA Cup semi-final and final, which meant the build-up was hectic. The major talking point for supporters was ticket allocation. The Football Association announced that 19,600 tickets would be available to Leeds United, prices ranging from £2 to £5. However, with an average home gate double the allocation figure, distribution as in previous finals would mean that many dedicated supporters would miss out. Sales on the black market soon saw tickets change hands for up to £200 as nobody wanted to miss out on the big day at Wembley.

As FA Cup final preparations developed, Leeds carried on their duel for the First Division crown with Derby, Manchester City and Liverpool. Revie's team lost a crucial encounter at Newcastle United three days after the semi-final win, Malcolm Macdonald scoring a late winner. The defeat saw a shift in odds at Corals. Derby County were new 5/4 favourites. Leeds went out to 3/1 with Liverpool second favourites at 7/4. In the FA Cup, Leeds were still quoted as 7/4 favourites with semi-final replay winners Arsenal 6/4. For the double, Leeds went out to 5/1.

Leeds redeemed themselves in their next outing at West Brom and in their penultimate league game, a home clash with to Chelsea. Leeds' victory at The Hawthorns came courtesy of a controversial Johnny Giles spot kick awarded after Jones was brought down inside the box, moments after Bremner was sandwiched by two West Brom defenders on the edge of the penalty box. Commenting on the key moment, Hugh Johns (*The People*) wrote:

The terrible strain of maintaining a challenge for soccer's top two prizes was etched deep in the tear-filled eyes of battling Billy Bremner when the goal that keeps Leeds in the championship race was scored. If there is one man in this superbly equipped Leeds line-up that Bremner can depend on in the stress situation of a penalty kick, it has got to be his midfield partner Giles. He is so ice-cool he could freeze a boiling kettle, but Bremner didn't dare look this time. Huddled on his haunches, his hands clasped in prayer, skipper Bremner turned his back on the action. Only when the roar of the travelling Elland Road supporters signalled Giles' fourth penalty this season did Bremner rise. Then he ran fully fifty yards, wreathed in smiles, to clasp Giles.

Following the win Don Revie said:

'After the disappointment of losing at Newcastle I was very pleased. The lads played some great stuff in a difficult swirling wind. The penalty, I didn't think it was controversial.'

Billy Bremner added:

'All the pressure in the world was on Johnny as he waited for David to be treated. I couldn't look but Johnny just placed the ball on the spot, runs a few spaces and tucks it in the net; that's professional.'

Leeds' 2-0 win against the Londoners, with goals from Bremner and Jones, aligned to Derby defeating Liverpool 1-0 was the right combination of results for the Yorkshire side because, no matter what Liverpool achieved in their last game at Arsenal, Leeds required a point from their clash at Wolves to claim the title. The league table read:

Derby County	P42	58 pts
Leeds United	P41	57 pts
Manchester City	P41	57 pts
Liverpool	P41	56 pts

Leeds' night of destiny, however, due to a Football Association ruling, would take place forty-eight hours after the FA Cup final against Arsenal, the same evening

Liverpool faced the Gunners. For United's squad there was a small matter of the double, which brought memories flooding back of the ill-fated double bid in 1965 and treble failure in 1970. Norman Hunter:

'I never slept a wink when Leeds played Liverpool. Coming up the tunnel onto the Wembley pitch was something I'd always dreamt about. You look for the family as you walk towards the centre circle, as it's something you have seen on television many times. I remember Sprakie playing brilliantly, the goals, but not much about the game; unfortunately, 1970 also ended in heartache. There was always one important game after another. Other teams rested players for a week or two, we didn't have such a luxury and all played with injuries. Don came to us all at times and you knew that you were not fit but he'd put his arm around you and say "I'd rather have a three-quarter fit you in the side". He generally used the same players and if anyone was injured Paul Madeley would step in and we'd swap around. Luckily for me, he slipped in at right-back or centre half. He was some player, different class.'

Paul Reaney:

'The Liverpool final was a blur; we were young kids playing a really good side. During the build-up, we went away but still didn't know what was going to hit us. I'll never forget that first roar when you walk out and look around. Wembley is packed and you don't know where to look. You wave to family as if you are in charge, but inside you are shaking like mad because

Bremner scores against Chelsea.

it is such a big occasion and you think, I'm at Wembley. We only had ten fit players, Albert struggled, and although Bobby tried to get us going and Billy got us back into the game it just wasn't our day.'

Paul Madeley:

'We played superbly against Chelsea and should have won. Eddie roasted David Webb on a terrible surface. By the end both teams settled for a replay but in the dressing room we could not believe we hadn't won. In the replay, we had our opportunities after Mick scored a super goal but you have to give them credit. Without making excuses, we lacked sharpness through these crucial games. You can do the running but mentally and physically your sharpness was hard to sustain over a long period of time. Pundits said we should concentrate on a specific tournament, but it just wasn't possible.'

Allan Clarke:

'Against Chelsea it was like playing in quicksand but we should have buried them. Unfortunately, Gary had a rush of blood and we failed to finish the chances we made. During the run-in of course tiredness crept in but you're in the semi-final of the FA Cup; you don't want to lose, you're second in the league; you want to keep the pressure up, you're then playing in a European Cup; you want to win that. Some people said we had a bad season, the majority of players would go though an entire career without coming close to what we achieved. We lost out, and I'm a terrible loser, but to be involved right to the death was fantastic; and we had season after season like that.'

Mick Jones:

'As a young boy my dream was to play in an FA Cup final, as a player it was one of my great ambitions. Against Chelsea when I scored I thought we'd won. I turned around, Don signalled eight minutes to go. Unfortunately, the match went into extra time. I was the first to go down with cramp; even Norman went down which shows how bad it was. As for the replay, naturally we were all distraught. We learned a lot that season even though it ended so disappointingly.'

Johnny Giles:

'Against Chelsea we should have won at Wembley, we were by far the better team. Gary slipped up and you cannot afford to give away easy goals in a tight game. What you have you hold and if they are going to score a goal it has to be a good one. At half-time, they were delighted because they knew they had got a hiding and they were on level terms. As a professional footballer, there is nothing better, because you know that you should be out of this game so have nothing to lose. The pitch was disgraceful but we did more than enough to win.'

Pop Idols!

Peter Lorimer:

'After the Chelsea game there was obvious disappointment because we had pulverised them at Wembley. Our play that day was probably the finest we played in any final, even though the pitch was bad. We dominated a very good Chelsea side and got enough goals to win but Gary had one of his days. We talked about winning the cup and thought we'd win it every year because we were better than the rest of the sides. The mystery is that we didn't win more. We all have our own opinions. For me, we were over-committed in competitions and our Achilles heel was we didn't use the squad. There were occasions when players needed a rest but we wanted to play and Don wanted us out there. Looking back, we should have used the squad more and the players who came in would have been up for it. There was also the travelling. Nowadays players are on the first direct flight home from Europe minutes after the game and would be back in the city. We would trail back on the Thursday from say East Germany on buses, planes, get back and be playing in London, so off we'd go again.'

There was little time to relax, but the players enjoyed the cup final traditions of recording a song and being measured for their matchday suit. *Leeds Leeds Leeds* was recorded in Manchester but is better known today as *Marching on Together*. Paul Madeley recalls:

'There were some horrible voices among the players, so the producers put in a couple of "ringers" to boost the vocals!'

Mick Jones added:

'None of the lads fancied standing in front of the microphone so I was pushed forward as lead singer, they said they'd back me up! It was great fun.'

As for the pear-coloured suits, Allan Clarke recalls:

'Billy and I watched Jonah being measured. When they asked him to measure his inside leg, the look on his face! Billy and I killed ourselves laughing!'

Numerous magazine and newspaper articles were published leading up to the final. Predictions were plentiful in *Goal's* cup final special. Editor Alan Hughes:

I'll risk spoiling a beautiful friendship with Highbury chief Bertie Mee by tipping Arsenal to lose the final. The choice of words is deliberate. Arsenal to lose, not Leeds to win because it is all going to turn in the Arsenal goalmouth where the London side go into their game of the season without their man of all seasons Bob Wilson. Leeds and Arsenal know each other well enough that Wilson's absence is enough to swing it, and anyway Leeds deserve to win the cup, surely.

The popular weekly magazine's cup final special.

Jimmy Hill:

I am certain it will be a very close game, but on balance I must favour Leeds. Terry Cooper's absence will not affect them with Paul Madeley in his place as much as Bob Wilson's absence will affect Arsenal. As for the score, it's 2-1 to Leeds but please don't put your shirt on it.

Ray Bradley:

Leeds United, technical soccer supremos of the seventies, are back at Wembley just as I predicted they would be last January. The most sophisticated team in Britain swept back to Wembley after efficiently disposing of Birmingham in the semi-final, now comes the crunch in the centenary of the most cherished cup as Leeds bid to add this trophy to the Elland Road sideboard for the first time in their history. United are a tasty team who have played some magnificent football this season. A superbly drilled side with all the skills fit to embellish this centenary celebration... I fancy them to make it third time lucky on Saturday. Only a victorious Leeds will really deserve to be compared with past giants like Real Madrid. For Leeds have to face the fact that three abortive attempts in seven years will ultimately be termed as failure, and the ambitious aristocrats of Elland Road are anything but failures.

As for regular footballer columnists, Bobby Charlton noted:

I go for Leeds quite simply because they are the best all-round team in the country... In the final analysis it could all depend on which team has withstood the ballyhoo and publicity that surrounds cup final teams at this stage of the season. The side that conquers its nerves quicker could well win. I think it will be Leeds.

A 'Wembley Ratings' chart by experts appraised Leeds United's squad.

Mick Bates: *Assessment: Ball skill 7, passing 7, defensive ability 7, attacking ability 7, temperament 7. Judgement: Good enough for most First Division clubs, so he's a good man to have in reserve.*

Billy Bremner: *Assessment: Ball skill 9, passing 9, defensive ability 8, attacking ability 9, temperament 7. Judgement: Brilliant skipper for club and country. Always rises to the big occasion. Watch him strike up a dominant partnership with Giles in Wembley's open spaces.*

Jack Charlton: *Assessment: Ball skill 6, passing 7, defensive ability 9, attacking ability 8, temperament 8. Judgement: A tower of strength for many years, but now inclined to make occasional errors. Yet he belies his years and is forever a threat at corners.*

Allan Clarke: *Assessment: Ball skill 8, passing 7, defensive ability 6, attacking ability 9, temperament 8. Judgement: Gets goals the quiet way. He just pops up when there's a chance and it's in the net. Elusive, cool to an extreme and dangerous.*

Johnny Giles: *Assessment: Ball skill 9, passing 10, defensive ability 7, attacking ability 9, temperament 8. Judgement: Outstanding in midfield and launching pad for the majority of United's attacks. Creates havoc with one long-penetrating inch-perfect pass.*

Eddie Gray: *Assessment: Ball skill 10, passing 8, defensive ability 6, attacking ability 9, temperament 9. Judgement: Back at his sensational best. A real headache for any defence as he proved against Chelsea in the FA Cup final two years ago. Can go past defenders on either side, a rare gift.*

David Harvey: *Assessment: Positioning 7, handling 8, agility 9, distribution 8, temperament 9. Judgement: Proved a capable deputy in the final replay two years ago and again in last month's semi-final. Leeds would hardly miss Sprake if Harvey could repeat this form.*

Norman Hunter: *Assessment: Ball skill 6, passing 8, defensive ability 9, attacking ability 7, temperament 8. Judgement: Iron man in the back four and one of the strongest tacklers in the game. He can be relied on when under pressure.*

Mick Jones: *Assessment: Ball skill 7, passing 7, defensive ability 6, attacking ability 9, temperament 9. Judgement: Powerful forward. Has had much to do with the scoring feats of Clarke and Lorimer this season and is now banging in a few goals himself. Strong, determined and a tireless worker up front.*

Joe Jordan: *Assessment: Ball skill 7, passing 7, defensive ability 7, attacking ability 7, temperament 8. Judgement: Promising forward who, if he learns from the more experienced men around him, could be a future winner.*

Peter Lorimer: *Assessment: Ball skill 8, passing 7, defensive ability 7, attacking ability 9, temperament 8. Judgement: Give him an inch and he'll take a mile. United's top marksman this season, with so many of his goals coming from thunderous strikes. Arsenal must be careful.*

Paul Madeley: *Assessment: Ball skill 8, passing 8, defensive ability 9, attacking ability 8, temperament 10. Judgement: His versatility, strength, unselfishness and ability make him one of the outstanding footballers in the country. Wherever he plays he'll do a great job.*

Paul Reaney: *Assessment: Ball skill 8, passing 8, defensive ability 9, attacking ability 7, temperament 9. Judgement: A full-back of real class and courage. He uses his speed to full advantage and is always looking for the chance to overlap down the right wing.*

Gary Sprake: *Assessment: Positioning 8, handling 8, agility 8, distribution 8, temperament 6. Judgement: His one big-let down is that he suffers from either big-time nerves or a jinx. Normally a safe, courageous keeper, he is prone to making costly mistakes at most inopportune moments.*

As for the *Shoot!* cup final special, columnist Bobby Moore noted:

Ability, form on the day, determination, character, perhaps even a slice of luck, these will be the factors that matter at Wembley on Saturday. On the face of it there's little to choose between the two teams. Both defences are very good, giving precious little away, and there are potential match-winners in either side. However, for my money this is a match that will be won and lost in midfield, where four top internationals will be battling for supremacy… I think that Giles and Bremner will come out on top and help to turn their team's other advantages into victory. Although both teams are very thorough, very professional, I believe Leeds' long years at the peak give them a clear edge in experience of big-match occasion matches. Most important of all, I reckon Don Revie's side are not only more spectacular, but also the better all-round team, just. I'm predicting a win for Leeds, but I don't expect there to be more than one goal in it at the finish, say 1-0 or 2-1.

In a players' vote by fourteen stars of the era, Leeds came out on top 10-4. Here are their views:

Tony Brown (West Brom): *I'm going for Arsenal. I think it will be a very close and exciting game, with the Gunners winning 2-1 and without the need for extra time. I'm tipping Arsenal because they've had no real pressures on them, while Leeds have been bidding for the league championship.*

Chris Lawler (Liverpool): *I think Leeds will win the FA Cup on Saturday because they've been well in form for weeks, whereas Arsenal haven't been at all impressive. The more I think about this game the more I'm convinced Leeds will do it. Yes, the Cup must go to Elland Road.*

Ron Davies (Southampton): *Leeds have been threatening to win the FA Cup for several seasons now, and this coming Saturday I expect them to achieve that ambition. Apart from that, they're more dangerous up front than Arsenal and liable to give the Gunners' rearguard a hectic time. I'd like to see plenty of goals because obviously it makes a game much more exciting, but I don't think they'll be much in it. 1-0 to Leeds is my forecast.*

Graham Cross (Leicester City): *Leeds will win the FA Cup, without a doubt. They're playing well, winning games convincingly, whereas Arsenal have been struggling a bit just recently. In fact, I thought the Gunners were fortunate to win their semi-final replay against Stoke at Goodison. Leeds don't need luck, they rely purely on skill. Once Don Revie's lads open their account they'll be no holding them. In fact, I reckon they'll win by three clear goals.*

Jimmy Robertson (Ipswich Town): *I think it will be a great final, although I can't see many goals being scored. Both teams have a lot of respect for each other and will be anxious not to give anything away at the back but I've fancied Arsenal all along in this cup competition and I'm still taking them to win.*

Rodney Marsh (Manchester City): *I tipped Arsenal to win the FA Cup before the semi-finals, so I see no reason to change my mind now. They seem better equipped for the occasion, with players who can raise their game. Leeds have faltered too often at this stage for my liking and its not because I'm from the South that I predict Arsenal will win by two goals.*

Tommy Wright (Everton): *If Billy Bremner and Johnny Giles hit top form, then I can't possibly see Arsenal winning. I would love Arsenal to win for my old teammate Alan Ball's sake. Leeds will be too strong in midfield and attack for the Gunners defence. Although it will be very close, it's Leeds by 2-1 for me.*

Ernie Hunt (Coventry City): *I don't like backing against Leeds, but I have a suspicion that Arsenal will win. For all Leeds' skills, its always in my mind that they could fail when the pressure is on. I think Ballie will give Arsenal the lift needed to win, but there will be no more than a goal between the clubs at the end, I'm sure.*

Billy Bonds (West Ham): *I must take Leeds United to beat Arsenal at Wembley on Saturday. This Leeds outfit are so strong in every department that I honestly can't see them losing out to the Gunners. A match-winner for Leeds, well, Mick Jones, Allan Clarke, Eddie Gray or Johnny Giles… you take your pick!*

Peter Bonetti (Chelsea): *I'm backing Leeds, not for sentimental reasons, such as because they've not won it before or because we stopped them in the 1970 final. No, they get my support for their ability to blend together and outstanding teamwork by brilliant players that deserve to triumph at Wembley on the big day.*

John Jackson (Crystal Palace): *The difference between the two finalists is consistency. Leeds are now able to sustain top performances week in, week out, while Arsenal are erratic in their play. I strongly favour Leeds to carry off the cup after a great match with a low scoreline, something like 1-0.*

David Wagstaffe (Wolves): *No problem, Leeds by 2-0 or 2-1. It's in midfield that they have the edge with Giles and Bremner so effective. Alan Ball may get so involved with this pair that his own game could suffer. Leeds deserve to win something this season, Arsenal took the lot last year! I see no reason why it shouldn't be a good game to watch. Both teams like to attack, I'm looking forward to it.*

Willie Morgan (Manchester United): *It's got to be Leeds. They're the best team in the country. They have so much all-round skill in their side, a skill Arsenal won't be able to match. As a professional myself, I've never seen a team play so well together and for each other. When Leeds turn it on they don't rely upon one or two individuals, they do it as a team. It'll be a good final, but it's going to be Leeds' cup.*

Colin Todd (Derby): *On paper it looks a very close match. Both teams have all-round strength, especially at the back but I think Leeds are more powerful up front where Eddie Gray could be a match-winner. Yes, I'm tipping Don Revie's side.*

Like its counterpart, *Shoot!* analysed the players in depth. This is how they rated the Leeds United players' strengths and weaknesses. Interestingly, David Harvey does not feature!

Gary Sprake: *Strengths: Impressive with his bravery at corners, reads the game well. Weaknesses: Loses concentration occasionally.*

Paul Reaney: *Strengths: Good marker, times his tackles well. Weaknesses: Slow at getting back into defence after overlapping.*

Paul Madeley: *Strengths: Can play in any position (except goal!). Weaknesses: Lack of speed.*

Billy Bremner: *Strengths: Non-stop energy, also has a habit of scoring vital goals. Weaknesses: His temperament!*

Jack Charlton: *Strengths: Commanding in the air, dangerous in attack. Weaknesses: Can be caught out of position.*

Norman Hunter: *Strengths: Tackles like a tank, covers like an army. Weaknesses: Critics say his right leg, but his teammates don't agree.*

Peter Lorimer: *Strengths: Reputed to have the hardest shot in soccer. Weaknesses: Not happy taking on a full-back.*

Allan Clarke: *Strengths: Always a threat in the penalty area, good in the air. Weaknesses: Sometimes fades during a game.*

Mick Jones: *Strengths: Good temperament for a striker, has an eye for goals. Weaknesses: Suspect ball control.*

Johnny Giles: *Strengths: Uncanny accuracy with his passing, good with both feet. Weaknesses: Sorry, but we can't see any.*

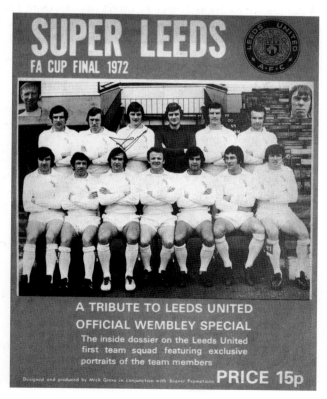

Leeds United's official commemorative brochure.

Eddie Gray: Strengths: Has the ability to beat defenders in mazy dribbles. Weaknesses: Occasionally he overruns the ball during those mazy runs.

Mick Bates: Strengths: Plays well when called on, despite inexperience. Weaknesses: Not a strong tackler.

If Leeds clinched the FA Cup, Don Revie would become the eighth man in history to gain a winners' medal as a player then manage an FA Cup-winning team, the others being Peter McWilliam, Billy Walker, Joe Smith, Jimmy Seed, Matt Busby, Joe Mercer and Bill Shankly. Derek Wallis (*Daily Mirror*):

Revie would be the last to dismiss Arsenal as opponents but he believes Leeds in form can beat any opposition. I believe so too. Yet I had great difficulty in making up my mind about this centenary final because Arsenal, having lost the first half of last season's double, will only grudgingly concede the cup as well. But I am convinced that Leeds have superior midfield players in Billy Bremner, Johnny Giles and Eddie Gray, and the attack, with the cunning of Allan Clarke, the strength of Mick Jones and the explosive shooting of Peter Lorimer, will make the greater impact.

James Mossop (*Sunday Express*) concurred with his fellow journalist's conclusion as to the destiny of the FA Cup. Mossop even predicted the hero in his weekly column's title: 'Clarke can win Cup Final for Leeds'. The columnist penned:

Sweet relief, I feel, will flow from Saturday's centenary final where Leeds will be striving for the form that captivated millions of armchair television fans earlier this season. Among those fireside thrills were three first-half goals against Arsenal... That 3-0 meeting at Elland Road will be too fresh in Arsenal minds to be irrelevant however. Leeds destroyed them in the first half and then rested on their lead, as simple as that.

The special atmosphere of Wembley can spur men to superhuman deeds. That famous stadium can also destroy as well. It ravaged Leeds in 1965 when they lost to Liverpool in extra time. Their big names forgot how to play, lesser men could not quell their butterflies... Seven years on Leeds are better, much better than two years ago when Chelsea beat them in a replayed final and Celtic defeated them in the semi-final of the European Cup. They now have the confidence, the skill and the poise to stroke their way through with a style that can make it one of the most memorable finals of all time.

Arsenal, last year's double champions, have to defeat Leeds in midfield if they are to stop that gallop but have in Peter Storey, Alan Ball and George Graham the command to run Billy Bremner, Johnny Giles and Eddie Gray out of it. The doubts, even if you live next door to Arsenal's Highbury home must be heavy. The telepathic understanding of Bremner and Giles is one of the mysteries of modern football and Wembley is made for the baffling talents of Eddie Gray.

The two crucial factors, which point to an Arsenal defeat, can be found in their defence and in Leeds' attack... Arsenal cannot possibly push up with the same assurance as if Bob Wilson was in goal. I wonder too whether their concern over Geoff Barnett (Wilson's understudy) will so effect Arsenal's concentration that the grip they need to keep on Allan Clarke will be relaxed.

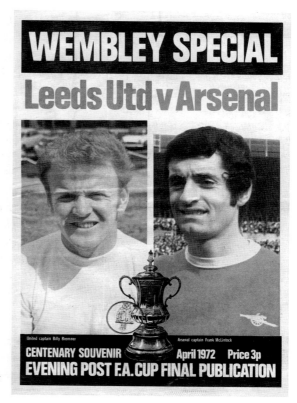

Yorkshire Evening Post
FA Cup final special.

This would be fatal. Sniffer is a ghost of a scorer, one mistake and he pounces, just as Jimmy Greaves used to do.

This final could be the platform for Clarke to launch himself as a player approaching the greatness that has been predicted for him. He is maturing now. Much more mature than when I saw him in the FA Cup final and European Cup semi-final games in 1970. Then I looked in vain for him to command the stage; to show us that he had all the presence and talent of a master player. It may have been nerves, fear or awe that affected him; his team suffered. That, however, was the Allan Clarke of yesteryear. The 1972 model carries his confidence through to arrogance. He struts the soccer fields of England, thrilling his own fans and annoying opponents. Clarke is the man who can win this 100th cup final, the man who can send Billy Bremner shooting up the red-carpeted stairs first to receive the FA Cup, the trophy Leeds United have never won.

The club's 'Official Wembley Special' gave a brief biography on each player. Among a host of 'useful' information, fans were informed about a player's most embarrassing moment, choice of car, favourite film and movie star, musical tastes, personal likes at breakfast and the biggest superstition. Interestingly, everyone ate Shredded Wheat for breakfast! As for favoured cars, Paul Reaney chose a Hillman Hunter, Billy Bremner a Toyota, Norman Hunter and Paul Madeley a Volvo, Peter Lorimer a Sunbeam

Alpine, Mick Jones a Vauxhall Ventora, Johnny Giles and David Harvey a Triumph Toledo and Eddie Gray a Wolseley.

For the final, Paul Madeley would be wearing yet another shirt. His record read: League Cup final 1968 (number nine), Fairs Cup final 1968 (number eight), FA Cup final 1970 (number two), Fairs Cup final 1971 (number eleven), FA Cup final 1972 (number three). Following his appearance at number five against Sunderland in 1973, Madeley was the most versatile cup finalist ever.

Local reporter Don Warters discussed the final in an *Evening Post* FA Cup publication:

I have little hesitation in describing United as the most exciting side around these days and I am not alone in this, for players with other clubs mention the millions of people who must have marvelled at United's brilliance on television. Although it is the players who make or break the club, Revie's drive and inspiration in the background has been a key factor in United's coming-of-age. He protects his players fiercely and sees they get the best treatment wherever they go and although nursing a back injury these days he rarely misses out on a training session.

This was illustrated as we talked in the warmth and luxurious comfort of his office at Elland Road on a bitterly cold day. With it snowing outside, I expressed my surprise that he had bothered to train with his players that foul morning. His reply was quick and cutting. 'I would not ask my players to do anything I would not be prepared to do myself. If I wanted to stay in a warm office while they slogged it out in the cold, I could do, but that is not my way. A manager's place is with his players and that is where I try to be at all times.'

It was typical of the huge appetite for the job he holds and does so well. His enthusiasm is still as great as it was in the early days and even now, after so long at the summit, he rarely arrives at the ground after 8.30 a.m. It is a dedication to duty that has clearly rubbed off on his players and is another reason why I regard United as a good bet to win the FA Cup this term for the first time in their history.

As the big day approached the Leeds squad followed a set routine. Allan Clarke:

'We travelled to London on the Thursday and stayed at the Hendon Hall Hotel. We trained at a local park to keep sharp. The sessions were very light, just stretching exercises to keep loose. I was doubtful along with Eddie Gray and Johnny Giles. I had a badly bruised ankle but obviously wanted to play. We had our fitness tests and passed. In any case the gaffer wanted us all to play. We had our usual game of bingo and carpet bowls before watching a video of our win over Southampton. We were relaxed and ready. One or two of the lads were a little apprehensive but the majority of the Leeds side was used to big occasions. The bigger the game the better we responded.'

Peter Lorimer:

'The manager took us away, but as the game approached, in training you think "I hope I don't pull a muscle". The five-a-sides became tame because the match is the next day. Like Paul Reaney in 1970, Terry Cooper broke a leg before a major final, which must have been a

nightmare. As with Paul against Chelsea, our feelings were for Terry because he had helped us get to the final.'

Helping the players relax was Don Revie's close friend Herbert Warner. Billy Bremner recalled:

'Herbert was great, a lovely feller. If there was any tension or the boys were a wee bit uptight before big matches you could take it out on Herbert, and most of the boys did. If he wasn't on a trip there was something missing, he was like one of the family. Herbert never took offence at any of our pranks.'

On FA Cup final day both managers gave comments. Don Revie:

'I hope we can make this final a game to remember. We shall go out to attack Arsenal. I have told the players we can make this a season of seasons, they are in the right frame of mind to go out there and put into practice what we know they are capable of. The players have showed they can keep on bouncing back. They have ability and experience and can go out there and play, I shall be disappointed if they don't. The players have found a new belief in themselves, something I have been telling them for years. This season they have really turned it on. I don't have to tell them what to do now, they know what is expected of them. They are full of confidence. The difference between this side and the 1970 one is that they believe in themselves more. There is so much at stake this weekend; if necessary, we shall give Johnny and Allan painkilling injections to get them out there to face Arsenal. I am determined to put out a full-strength side at Wembley.'

Bertie Mee:

'I have never known us to be so relaxed, there has almost been a holiday atmosphere at our training camp near Bournemouth. There is not going to be any team talk tomorrow, we don't need one, every player knows exactly what he has got to do. I am not going to make any rash forecasts but we are in confident mood, we expect to see the trophy back on the sideboard on Monday.'

Come Saturday morning, for armchair supporters the choice was Frank Bough's *Cup Final Grandstand* or Dickie Davies's *World of Sport*. These offered similar fare, such as meet the players, how the teams reached Wembley, and endless interviews. *Cup Final Grandstand* included highlights of *Cup Final It's a Knockout* introduced by Stuart Hall and Eddie Waring. The event, between supporters of both clubs, took place in Congleton, Cheshire, a week before the final. On the morning of the match, Allan Clarke recalls:

'The gaffer was determined to keep our routine the same. We walked around Hendon Hall's grounds then came back for our pre-match meal. We then watched a bit of Cup Final Grandstand before his main team talk. We went through the dossier of Arsenal players and game tactics. Then he announced the side. After the team talk, we set off for Wembley. When

the coach turned into Wembley Way, it was a fantastic sight. Wembley is a sensational stadium to play at. We had a walk on the pitch and waved to the supporters. I checked both penalty areas for divots. On our way to the changing rooms the television reporters interviewed us. It was a fantastic atmosphere.'

Johnny Giles:

'Naturally we were well aware of the occasion, it was not just another game, but once we were in the dressing room it was business as usual. The shirts were lined out in order, one to twelve, and each player prepared in their normal manner.'

Paul Reaney:

'We had been there before so knew what to expect. It was Wembley and you have the crowd but you can't let that take over the build-up. The game is not fear, more apprehension. The pre-match team talk was at the hotel because at Wembley so much happens. You see all the fans on Wembley Way, go on the pitch and soak in the atmosphere. You are now ready to play, not particularly talk, in the dressing room. Don gave more words of encouragement than anything else because you just want to get out there and fly. He said as before every game, confidence and concentration.'

Billy Bremner:

'We'd already had our main team talk at the hotel so the gaffer just reiterated a few key points. I remember he reminded us one final time of the Chelsea game when we let ourselves down. Not that we really needed reminding, we knew what was expected of us.'

Soon it was time to leave the sanctuary of the dressing room. Allan Clarke:

'When we came out of the changing room it was tense. I had a chat to Alan Ball and I remember Peter Simpson looking at me trying to psyche me out, and I remember thinking, "this is it".'

Paul Madeley:

'Waiting was the worst part but the adrenaline rush and noise from the crowd when we emerged was incredible. I was sixth out after Norman and my stomach was going like hell; I just wanted to get on with it. I've often joked that it was nearly bad enough to turn round and go back in again!'

Mick Jones:

'Standing in the tunnel was really nerve-wracking. Standing there, all you see is a little light in the distance. As you walk towards it, it gets bigger and wider. Coming out of the tunnel the roar is unbelievable. After meeting the dignitaries we ran off for the kick-in and all my nerves disappeared.'

10

Cup Glory

Fifteen clubs entered the first FA Cup competition in 1871/72. The knockout tournament was the brainchild of Football Association secretary Charles Alcock. He stated at a meeting in the offices of London newspaper *The Sportsman*: 'It is desirable that a Challenge Cup shall be established in connection with the Association.'

Based at Wembley Stadium since 1923, many of the greatest shocks in David *v.* Goliath clashes and iconic images had been created in the competition, especially at the Twin Towers. The 1872 final at The Oval between The Wanderers, captained by Alcock, and Royal Engineers drew an attendance of 2,000 spectators. There were no nets and a rope served as a crossbar. The Engineers won 1–0. One century on, a capacity crowd of 100,000 paid £191,197 for the privilege. Worldwide 400 million

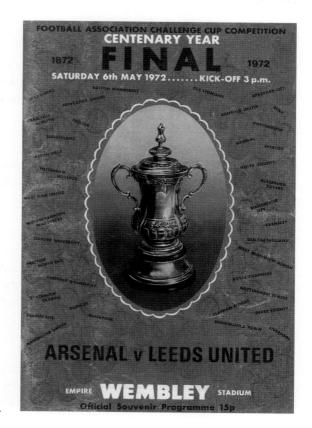

Destiny awaits.

117

LEEDS UTD
F.A. CUP WINNERS 1972

MILETA
SPORTS PRODUCT

CENTENARY
F.A. CUP FINAL 1972

3

LEEDS UNITED A.F.C.

THE EMPIRE STADIUM - WEMBLEY

The Football Association
Challenge Cup
Competition

FINAL
TIE

SAT., MAY 6, 1972

LEEDS UNITED A.F.C. LTD.

TURNSTILES

A

ENTRANCE

22

KICK-OFF 3 p.m.
YOU ARE ADVISED TO TAKE UP
YOUR POSITION BY 2.30 p.m.

837

EAST
STANDING
ENCLOSURE

CHAIRMAN:
WEMBLEY STADIUM LTD

STANDING
£1.00

TO BE RETAINED   (SEE PLAN AND CONDITIONS ON BACK)

Bremner and McLintock find time for a joke despite the tension.

people from forty-five countries watched the action. During the build-up Billy Bremner was quoted as saying that he would swap his league championship, Fairs Cup and League Cup winners' medals for a place in an FA Cup-winning side. Whether he was talking tongue-in-cheek or meant it literally is debatable, but it demonstrates the esteem the tournament was held in. The competition had an aura about it. Not only the oldest football competition in the world, it was English football's showpiece and, during the season, the BBC published a top-ten list of the biggest audiences for single programmes of British television. The FA Cup final featured four times!

Billy is introduced to HRH The Duke of Edinburgh.

Leeds and Arsenal would be competing for the third version of the trophy. The latest model weighed 175oz, was 19 inches tall and was ordered from Fattorini and Sons of Bradford. The schedule before kick-off included marching bands and a pageant of past FA Cup winners to mark the centenary of the competition. The teams, led out by managers Bertie Mee and Don Revie, passed through a 'guard of honour' of pageant representatives on the traditional walk to the halfway line in front of the Royal Box. After introductions to the Duke of Edinburgh and dignitaries, and the national anthem, the Leeds team warmed up at the tunnel end. Leeds, 13/8 favourites, as expected fielded Allan Clarke, Johnny Giles and Eddie Gray. Arsenal had one enforced change, Geoff Barnett deputising for Bob Wilson. Billy Bremner elected for the teams to stay as they were following the toss.

In an explosive opening minute, Clarke was penalised for fouling Alan Ball and Bob McNab was booked for a late tackle on Peter Lorimer, who resumed after treatment. The game's opening chance fell to Arsenal on seventeen minutes when Norman Hunter brought George down on the edge of the penalty area. From the resultant free-kick, Frank McLintock's low shot brought a sharp save from David Harvey.

Harvey recalls:

'I never saw McLintock's shot until it was almost on top of me. I was a bit lucky. I caught it between my face, shoulder and hands. It could have gone anywhere.'

Bremner added:

'McLintock hit one early doors and young 'un (Harvey) did enough. It took a wee swerve just as it came to him and he had to quickly change direction. Fortunately, he saved it. That was crucial. Who knows how the game would have gone if that had gone in? The first goal is so important.'

Just past the half-hour mark, Jack Charlton conceded a corner kick, following a probing pass by Ball. The England midfielder connected perfectly with an inch-perfect cross from George Armstrong to the edge of the 'D' to thunder a right-footed volley towards goal. Fortunately, for Leeds, Paul Reaney was on hand to hack the ball off the line. He recalls:

'I was always on the goal line for corner kicks. This time I saw the ball really late and just managed to get a boot to it. My instinct to drop back to the goal line developed from my early years at Leeds. Don Revie encouraged me to make it a part of my natural game.'

Although the Gunners had created more clear-cut chances, Leeds had been controlling possession and almost snatched the lead on thirty-seven minutes from a free-kick when Peter Storey fouled Clarke on the edge of the penalty box. As players jostled in the wall, Giles' misplaced pass rebounded to Lorimer and his instinctive twenty-yard strike was only just fumbled around the post by Barnett, who dropped the resultant corner but Leeds failed to capitalise. Soon Mick Jones had an effort scrape past the post, and then on the stroke of half-time Clarke was inches away from scoring following a flowing move that culminated in Bremner heading the ball into the penalty box. From McNab's attempted clearance Lorimer, on the edge of the area, instinctively hit a cross-shot across the face of the goal. Clarke on the far post acrobatically stooped to loop a header over Barnett, only to see it strike the crossbar. He recalls:

'Peter's shot that came towards me at the back stick. I'm amazed it didn't knock my head off but somehow my header dropped on top of the bar, it was close.'

The Leeds striker's effort was the closest his side had come to breaking the deadlock. There was still time for Bremner to receive a caution for dissent in injury time after the referee refused Leeds a corner, but although no goals had been scored Leeds had edged the opening period. Clarke recalls:

'The gaffer told us to just carry on as we were. We had been the better side and felt the goal would come eventually. The weather was red-hot and, although I was fit, after five or ten

minutes I was thinking "Christ, I need another lung here", but then I got my second wind and was fine.'

Eight minutes into the second half Leeds finally edged ahead with a terrific header from Clarke, who takes up the story:

'A ball was played towards me near the halfway line. McLintock was marking me. As I attempted to get away he pushed me. I tried to stay on my feet but actually fell over; Frank trod on my fingers, it didn't half hurt. Ball got the ball and played it forward; Big Jack intercepted it. We were now on the attack. Jack gave the ball to Paul (Madeley) who played a simple pass forward to Peter. I remember Billy passing me to join the attack. Peter played it to Jonah down the right flank, and I thought, "I've got to get into the box here". As Jonah took on McNab, I was on the edge of the box. He worked marvels and crossed the ball. As it was coming towards me I thought volley, right-foot volley, and I fancied it. Then all of a sudden as the ball's coming towards me it started to dip, and I realised it isn't going to reach me, so I thought "dive". You only have a second to make your mind up so I just took off and headed it. I knew it was going in, and obviously it fitted in the corner just nicely. Over the years I've lost count of how many people have asked me about the goal and introduced me to their children

Opposite: Allan heads home the most famous goal in Leeds United's history.

Right: Revie urges his Leeds team on.

who weren't even born in 1972. It means so much to so many Leeds United supporters, it's a very special memory in my footballing career. Even now when we play Arsenal at Elland Road supporters sing "Who put the ball in the Arsenal net? Allan Allan… Who put the ball in the Arsenal net? Allan Allan Clarke'; and that's a wonderful feeling.'

Mick Jones, whose cross proved vital, recalls:

'As I approached Arsenal's full-back McNab, I decided to take him on and get to the byline. Going past him I had a little bit of luck because the ball ricocheted off his legs and bobbled the right way for me. McNab knew it was a dangerous attacking position; he muttered in no uncertain terms how lucky I was! When I was in this situation I always aimed for the penalty spot. The ball was away from the goalkeeper's reach, and with defenders running back towards their goal anything could happen. I whipped in a good cross, Clarkie came flying in, he was going to volley the ball, but the ball dipped at the last moment, so he dived instead. He got a perfect connection and it fitted perfectly in the far corner. Allan came running over to celebrate and all the lads joined in. It was a fantastic feeling. Jogging back to the centre circle I realised there was a long way to go. Both teams would get chances to score, but deep down I knew we had a great chance because I couldn't see our defence letting them back into the game.'

Billy Bremner was convinced the goal would prove crucial:

'McNab was a wee bit unlucky, he's been criticised a lot for it, but as a defender you have to make up your mind whether you are going to dive for it, and he did. Jonah just got a break on him and cut a great ball in, and Clarkie headed a magnificent goal. When we went one up I felt, because it had been so tight, that this goal was going to be enough for us.'

Norman Hunter added:

'I was convinced Jonah had crossed it too early, but he didn't, Allan finished brilliantly. When it went in I raced half the length of the pitch before jumping on top of everyone.'

Arsenal had to respond and almost grabbed an equaliser on seventy-one minutes when George, quiet throughout, reacted instinctively to a loose ball near the penalty spot following a shot by Ball. Fortunately for Leeds, his hooked shot crashed against the crossbar and rebounded to safety with Harvey beaten. Billy Bremner recalled:

'George froze a bit on the day until he hit this great volley out of the blue, like from nothing, and it struck the crossbar and came flying out. This was the moment I knew it was going to be our day. You need a little bit of luck when you're playing against a side like Arsenal. We had it when George struck the bar.'

Norman Hunter added:

'Someone suggested we were a bit slack to let him have a shot. That's ridiculous. Give the lad credit, he seized the chance and whacked it, you can't do anything about shots like that.'

The Arsenal boss replaced John Radford with Ray Kennedy seventeen minutes from time but the Leeds defence could sense victory and stood firm. Indeed, they came closer to scoring late on when Charlton headed over from a corner, Lorimer struck a post from an angled drive and Gray shot wide when well placed after a mazy run. As Leeds' fans whistled for the referee to end the game the match had one final twist as Jones raced towards goal. He recalls:

'We had a signal from the bench that there was not too long remaining when suddenly a ball was played through to me in a dangerous position. I went past Peter Simpson and saw Arsenal's 'keeper Geoff Barnett come out to narrow the angle; I had a half-chance to score. I tried to nick the ball past him, but tumbled over the top of him and automatically put my left arm down to break my fall. The pain was unbearable. Unbeknown to me I'd dislocated my elbow. On any other pitch this injury would not have occurred. Throughout my career I had similar falls without any problems, the soft Wembley pitch caused the damage. I could hear Barnett saying, "get up you soft so and so", but he soon realised I wasn't joking because I was screaming in pain.'

Barnett played the goal kick short to Simpson but Charlton cleared his long ball as the referee signalled the end of the match. Don Revie's Leeds United had at last won the FA Cup. Billy Bremner recalls:

'My first thoughts were for the lads that we'd done it. Then I thought about the gaffer and looked for him. He was ecstatic and I thought "terrific, I'm delighted for you". I would have hated him to go through his time with Leeds as manager and not won the FA Cup.'

As United players celebrated, lying motionless on the ground still was Jones, being attended by Les Cocker and the club's medic Doc Adams. Allan Clarke recalls:

'I remember Norman coming over and we hugged, then the other lads. All of a sudden, I calmed down and noticed Mick still lying in Arsenal's penalty area. I remember Mick going down but didn't realise the extent of the injury. I went over, it was a sickening injury caused by a freak accident. For him to miss the celebrations was very upsetting. I was then told to join the lads who were lining up to get our medals.'

At last, after receiving runners-up medals following defeats against Liverpool and Chelsea, Billy Bremner had the opportunity receive his winners' medal and lift the much-coveted trophy. He recalled:

'When I went up to receive the FA Cup, daft as it seems, I remember thinking about Bobby Moore wiping his hands before receiving the World Cup from the Queen. I thought, "how could you remember to do that after you've just won the World Cup?" I thought he must have been so calm to think about something like that. So I told myself don't be going crazy, take your time and don't be desperate to turn round with the trophy, but you do, you turn round too quick, you're so keen to show the fans the trophy. My only wish is that I would have handed it back and let all the boys have a touch of it there and then. But at the time I thought, "nae bugger's getting hold of this. I'm away down the stairs with it, I'll give someone the base."'

Charlton took the base, then Giles, Reaney, Madeley, Hunter, Gray, Harvey, Lorimer, Clarke and finally substitute Bates, who collected Jones' medal, followed United's skipper to receive their cup winners' medals. In the meantime, Leeds' supporters recognised their hero was badly hurt and could be heard chanting: 'M.I. M.I... M.I.C... M.I.C.K... Mick Jones!' repeatedly. Determined to receive his medal, a heavily strapped Jones walked gingerly across the Wembley pitch to the Royal Box. He recalls:

'Les and Doc Adams told me I'd have to be carried off straight to the dressing room. I told them "no way". I realised we'd won the FA Cup and wanted to receive my medal from the Queen. As a player, one of my greatest ambitions was to receive a cup winners' medal and no injury was going to stop me. I told them to get me on my feet; I'd manage to walk across. Eventually they agreed but Doc Adams insisted on coming with me. After they strapped my

Billy lifts the FA Cup.

arm around my body, I slowly got up and began to walk across the pitch. I thought I'd collapse. I had no idea that Billy had already collected the FA Cup and the lads had been up for their medals. I was just determined to climb the Royal Box to receive my medal from the Queen. I only found out later that I'd kept her waiting for ten minutes. As we got to the bottom of the steps Mick Bates came over and told me he had my medal, but I still wanted to meet the Queen. I could just see Glenis and all the families on the right-hand side. Norman came over and helped me up the steps. Everyone was slinging their arms around me; Glenis was in tears. At the top of the stairs, again I nearly collapsed. We walked across the Royal Box and everyone shook my hand. When I approached the Queen I heard her say that she had nothing to give me. She shook my hand and asked me how I was. I felt awful, but fortunately, I was still in enough control to give her a polite reply! We walked to the end of the Royal Box and had to *stand for the national anthem. Once again I thought I was going to collapse. Somehow, I got to the bottom of the stairs where Doc Adams and the ambulance men were waiting with a stretcher. When we approached the tunnel end where the Leeds fans were situated, the reception was unbelievable. The supporters were chanting my name "M.I... M.I.C... M.I.C.K... Mick Jones!" I'll never forget it. We got to the dressing room and I rested on the treatment table. They needed four doctors to put my arm back into place. Two stood at the bottom and two at the top, I could feel my elbow snap back in.'*

After posing for photographs, Bremner led his team on a four-minute lap of honour. Leeds' fans were exultant, singing *When the Whites Go Marching In, Super Leeds, We Won the Cup* and *Leeds Leeds Leeds*. The loudest cheer was reserved when Revie held the cup aloft with Bremner, who carried the trophy off the pitch with *Revie's Aces* ringing in their ears. During post-match interviews, Don Revie said:

'I've waited years for this day. My Man of the Match was Norman Hunter. Every coach in the country will tell you he's brilliant, I reckon he's one of the greatest players who ever lived. This is the second happiest day of my life. The first was when we drew at Liverpool to win the League Championship in 1969, and now taking the FA Cup is marvellous. I don't think the ghost of their past performances worried the players at Wembley. I was particularly pleased with the way we played in the second half, and I must say that Clarke took his goal with terrific coolness. He had a look and picked his spot. The most difficult task I had before the final was

Allan with his 'Man of the Match'
award and the lid of the FA Cup!

telling one of my goalkeepers he would not be playing. After all, Gary has been our regular goalkeeper for eight or nine years and it must have been a big disappointment when I told him David would keep his place, but Gary was tremendous, he accepted the decision, another example of how close-knit our family is. Considering it was the first time David had played at Wembley he was magnificent. He has played well since coming into the side when Gary was injured a few weeks ago, so I decided I could not leave him out.'

Bertie Mee:

'It was a disappointing game; we didn't allow each other to play. Our teams can be likened to boxers whose styles just don't mix. There was little in it until the goal. Geoff Barnett had a great game. After the pressure he had been under he came through with flying colours. He did exceptionally well and he certainly has no cause to blame himself for the goal.'

The general consensus among the media was that the better team won. Hugh McIlvanney (*The Observer*):

Don Revie's Leeds United, the team who had come to regard Wembley as a place of near misses, won the FA Cup at their third attempt yesterday, when they outplayed Arsenal to an extent that was inadequately reflected in the scoreline. It was Leeds whose football was more controlled, whose ideas the more inventive. Once Leeds had settled, and especially after their goal, they dominated Arsenal confidently.

GREEN POST

SATURDAY MAY 6 1972   No. 26,984   Tel: LEEDS 32701   Price 3p.

Leeds United supporters with plenty to shout about in Trafalgar Square.

IT'S YOURS, UNITED

Free transfer for cup hero and Storrie

On Cup Final day, one of its past heroes has learned that he is being offered a free transfer.

Mike Trebilcock, the Portsmouth forward who scored two goals for Everton in the 1966 Final and joined Portsmouth five years later for £40,000 is one of four players being given free transfers. The others are reserve keeper Jim Middleton, Tommy Youlden, Leeds United player Jim Storrie and Mike Travers.

FRANCIS ACCEPTS

Former Leeds RL coach Roy Francis today accepted the post of team manager of Hull and will be in complete control.

Geoff Barnett, Arsenal goalkeeper, saves from Mick Jones, Leeds United centre-forward, in the Cup Final at Wembley. The United players on the left are Peter Lorimer and Allan Clarke.

Reaney 'rescue act' yet again

By MIKE CASEY

Neither Leeds United nor Arsenal could complain at the 68 half time score in a fiercely fought F.A. Cup Final. But some of the players must have blushed as they entered the dressing room as they reflected on how brilliantly which had produced countless free kicks.

The opening 10 minutes were a mixture of niggling tackles and misplaced passes as both teams tried to find their feet.

Even after referee David Smith had shown he intended to keep the game under control by booking Arsenal's Huddersfield-born full-back Bob McNab for a foul on Peter Lorimer in the first minute, play continued to be scrappy.

Apart from a long-range effort by George Graham, which went over the bar, United, obviously keen to carry out manager Don Revie's orders to "attack," were finding Arsenal skipper Frank McLintock and his colleagues a formidable barrier.

When Bremner's name was tackling defender Peter Storey keeping a tight grip on schemer Johnny Giles, the little Irishman was finding life tough.

Few chances

Gradually, Giles and his captain Billy Bremner gained midfield supremacy, but United's front-runners were finding few chances to show their mettle.

Arsenal's defence looked as solid as their reputation: their back four, McLintock, Peter Simpson, Storey and Pat Rice, were performing admirably.

Indeed, former Scottish international McLintock took time off from his defensive duties to lash in a fourteen header shot which David Harvey turned brilliantly by diving to his left.

For a time United had to defend when that touch little Geordie, George Armstrong made full use of the space left him by a strangely lax United defence.

Desperate lunge

Leeds, although on top on points, were lucky not to fall behind in the 30th minute when a flurry shot by Alan Ball was cleared

sad reading for a final which had promised to be a classic.

United's morale, which had been severely tested in a torrid first-half, was given the boost it needed right minutes after the restart.

Lorimer released Mick Jones with a smart pass which the hard working centre-forward turned in to a goal.

He lofted the ball to ALLAN CLARKE and the other half of United's £350,000 spearhead leapt high to power the ball into Barnett's net.

The title had turned United's way and they began to pulverise the Gunner's defence.

Conteh sprints to hat-trick

Anu Conteh completed a fine hat-trick when he won the 100 metres for the third successive year, in the Varsity athletics match at Crystal Palace today.

Conteh, a law student at Cambridge, romped away in 10.0 seconds. He finished a fifth of a second ahead of Oxford's Stephen White, with David Roberts (Cambridge) third in 11.4sec.

Death ends family Cup Final plan

Tragedy hit a Yorkshire family's plans to see the F.A. Cup Final at Wembley today when one of them died in a car accident in Gelderd Road, Birstall, near Leeds.

Two brothers, Mr. John Francis Bevins (34) and Mr. David Bevins (21), had planned to go to Wembley today with their father, Mr. Frank Bevins, Alberton Grange Rise, Moortown, Leeds.

The brothers, were each driving to the family home from their work last night. John was an international research mathematician at ICI, Isle (Cheshire).

SAW CRASHED CAR

David, a trainee manager with a firm of wholesale newsagents in Warrington, said today that he and John came home almost every weekend to see with their parents, Mr. Bevins and his wife Betty. Mr. Bevins is a messenger at Rushsfbar Road, Barnsbely, Leeds.

Near the Cash and Six H.....s, Birstall, John's sports car was involved in a crash on the way killed.

David came upon the scene of the accident, and realised that the crash victim was his brother.

John was an international research mathematician at ICI, Isle (Cheshire).

"There was nothing I could do," he said. "They had already taken him to hospital and I went to identify him."

Clarke header brings Cup to Elland Road: 1-0

CUP WINNERS AT LAST! LEEDS UNITED WON THE F.A. CUP CENTENARY FINAL AGAINST ARSENAL AT WEMBLEY BY 1-0.

Allan Clarke headed the vital goal from Mick Jones's precision pass after 53 minutes. There were four bookings—McNab and George (Arsenal), Hunter and Bremner (Leeds).

Leeds: Harvey, Reaney, Cooper, Bremner, Charlton, Hunter, Lorimer, Clarke, Jones, Giles, Madeley. Sub: Bates.

Arsenal: Barnett, Rice, McNab, Storey, McLintock, Simpson, Armstrong, Ball, Radford, George, Graham. Sub: Kennedy.

By DON WARTERS

Leeds', goalkeeper David Harvey, who has been so impressive in United's last five matches after coming into the side when Welsh international Gary Sprake was injured, kept his place for today's big game.

He was the only member of the Leeds United side not to have played at Wembley although he did keep goal when Chelsea beat United in the 1970 F.A. Cup Final replay at the Stadford.

There was good news for United when Johnny Giles passed a late fitness test and, like United's other doubtful starter, Allan Clarke, took the field without any pain-killing injections.

The Arsenal side was announced yesterday with Charlie George at centre-forward. John Radford and Goole-forward and Ray Kennedy substitute.

Receipts of £198,000 were a record for the F.A. Cup Final at Wembley, beating by £4,000 those far last year's Final between Arsenal and Liverpool.

GANTON TURF

The pitch was in excellent condition, the lush green turf at scene of it from Ganton Golf Club, Yorkshire — providing a top contrast to the bare and sandy surface which United had to play on in the 1970 Final.

The game was only 60 seconds old when referee Smith made it plain he was going to keep a firm hold on matters. He booked Arsenal full-back McNab for a tackle on Lorimer on the touchline in front of the Royal box, from which the Queen and the Duke of Edinburgh were watching.

First shot of goal came a couple of minutes later from Arsenal's Graham 20 yards out, but the ball sailed over the bar.

GRAY GROUNDED

When United tried to make progress on the left Gray was twice grounded unfairly. Charlton committed the next foul, but Harvey gathered Simpson's free kick confidently.

Neither side had yet settled down as these tense opening minutes ticked by and several passes on both sides went astray.

As expected, Harvey was keeping a close watch on Giles in an effort to prevent United's midfield ace from getting a grip as midfield but when Harvey got the ball he sometimes spray-passed the left of the goal, but the latter's header, although pouring over Barnett across the bar and was cleared.

The third booking of the game came just on half-time and it was United skipper Bremner whose name was

taken apparently for arguing with the referee. It was Bremner's fourth booking of the season.

Half-time:

Arsenal 0
Leeds United .. 0

The booking scores were levelled a minute into the second half when Mr. Smith cautioned George, who had apparently said something to the official shortly after being booked for a foul on Bremner.

GRAY'S CHASE

An encouraging move by United looked dangerous when Gray chased a ball to the bye-line, but it pulled back from over the line before he could turn it in to the middle.

Arsenal made precious down the right and when Armstrong put a centre over to the far side of the goal the full-back McNab rose up to connect with a header but put the ball into the side netting.

United who had looked a shade the more relaxed side in this half, went away to take the lead in the 53rd minute with a well engineered and firmly executed goal.

Lorimer supplied Jones with a fine pass on to the right of the penalty area and United's big centre-forward crossed he measured to precision CLARKE with the opportunity to head it home from some 16 yards out and the latter made no mistake.

He stamped low to head the ball out of Barnett's reach and into the goal near the right-hand post.

ENCOURAGED

The goal gave United encouragement they needed and there was a great deal more confidence now about their play.

Lorimer found well to get through Arsenal's strong defence and even though he was held back by his shirt he snatched a shot which went over the bar but the referee had already blown to award United a free kick.

Lorimer got a second chance when the ball was tapped to him but again shot over.

Bremner came in the some special attention from Ball when the two players clashed on the far transition during which the fiery Arsenal man had three attempts to tackle Bremner from behind before the United skipper actually went down.

The referee gave Ball a final lecture for his misadventure.

Armstrong tried hard to set and set George get his chance but the long-barrel Arsenal defence was getting on top near to Harvey most of their moves petered out on the edge of the line in the final whistle.

In one move McNab did manage to get in a shot but it barely troubled United's goalkeeper.

Bremner had attention from trainer Les Cocker when he was brought down, while potentially his way through near the edge of the penalty area but he was able to resume after treatment.

Cricket scores

Aussie Soccer Results

Frank McGhee (*Sunday Mirror*):

Arsenal could have tried for another 100 years and still would not have a serious chance of beating Leeds. Not on the form, the mood and the manpower seen in this centenary cup final.

Alan Hoby (*Sunday Express*):

The elegant stylists of Leeds have won the FA Cup for the first time. Whatever happens the beaten finalists of 1965 and 1970 have at last killed the sneer that they always stumble at the final hurdle. That taunt lies buried forever beneath the damp green turf of Wembley.

David Miller (*Sunday Telegraph*):

Leeds, the most consistent team in European soccer for the last eight years, carried off the centenary FA Cup in a final that was eventually one-sided. From the start Leeds were transparently the better side and by the finish they had outplayed the opposition in almost every phase of the game, even if they only controlled it for that last half-hour.

Albert Barham (*The Guardian*):

A new name, Leeds United, will be inscribed on the plinth of the FA Cup this centenary year and few will deny that the honour has been long overdue. A spectacularly headed goal by Clarke was insufficient reward for the superiority of Leeds in every department of the game. They could and should have had a couple more afterwards.

Frank Butler (*News of the World*):

Don Revie, superstitious manager of the most superstitious team in the world, can throw away his old suits and go on a shopping spree on Saville Row. For it was third time lucky for the mighty Yorkshire giants. Leeds well deserved their victory after they got out of the Yale-lock grip of the Arsenal defensive system in the first half. A goal was needed to break the Arsenal system and what a great goal Leeds scored. Clarke took it perfectly with his head and Barnett was nowhere near when the ball crossed the line. Leeds had always looked the more classy footballing side. Once they scored they blossomed out like superman. Suddenly Arsenal looked tired, beaten and very ordinary.

Terry Brindle (*Yorkshire Post*):

It was the day on which Leeds United proved beyond question that they are a great side. A day on which the most coveted trophy in soccer was added to their impressive pedigree, and no side that has not won the cup can claim to true greatness.

Don Warters (*Evening Post*):

Hail Leeds United! Don Revie's heroes won the FA Cup in its centenary year with a mixture of skill, guts and indomitable spirit, and let no one say that the Elland Road men did not deserve the glory. United's second half superiority could have brought more goals. Yet this was United's day. It might not have been their most attractive performance of the season, but it was a skilfully controlled and super-efficient display, one which proved too good on the day for Arsenal.

Mike Casey, Sports Editor, (*Evening Post*):

Allan Clarke, his face drawn with emotion, his hands tightly clutching his first FA Cup winners' medal and second Wembley 'Man of the Match' award, warily pushed his way through the throng of well-wishers in Leeds United's dressing room after Saturday's centenary final. Shrugging off the well-intentioned handshakes and words of congratulations, the tall England striker who, less than an hour earlier, had headed the goal that brought the coveted trophy to Elland Road for the first time in the club's history, made anxiously for the prone figure on the wooden bench in the corner. 'How do you feel?' he asked as he squatted down besides his injured colleague, centre forward Mick Jones. The stricken star, his left arm strapped to his chest, whispered an unconvincing reassurance before another wave of pain swept the faint smile from his ashen face. Clarke, oblivious to the restrained celebrations going on around him, the traditional drinking of champagne from soccer's most famous trophy, was conscious only of his friend's misery. Jones, the man they say takes most of the punishment to allow the lethal Clarke more time and space in which to exercise his goal-scoring ability, was hurt. The roar of the 100,000 crowd; the thrill of scoring the winner at Wembley, all were pushed to the back of Clarke's mind as he tried to comfort his friend and colleague. This was not a world-class footballer seeking to improve his image. This was a deed performed, as far as Clarke was concerned, and in the privacy of an ordinary untidy dressing room, reeking with the smell of liniment and littered with the paraphernalia which accompanies the game. The fact that it occurred on the most important day in the English soccer calendar only 100 yards or so away from the monarch was coincidental. It merely added to the drama of an emotion-packed afternoon. Clarke's reaction would have been the same any day of the year. It proved to me that

WE'VE WON IT!

LEEDS UNITED'S CUP HEROES . . . .

The moment a city had been waiting for . . . Leeds United with the major trophy they have earned so well in beating Arsenal 1—0.

From left to right are: Mick Bates, Paul Madeley, Eddie Gray, Paul Reaney, Johnny Giles, Jack Charlton, Alan Clarke, Billy Bremner, Peter Lorimer, Norman Hunter and David Harvey.

. . . AND THE MAN WHO MISSED THIS HISTORIC PICTURE.

Mick Jones, the man with the big heart who made United's goal, ended the match writhing in agony in the Arsenal penalty area.

His elbow had been dislocated in collision with the Arsenal goalkeeper. United trainer Les Cocker told him the match was over and he had a Cup winner's medal as he lay on the turf. He was then carried off on a stretcher, but made a lone brave walk up to the Royal box where the Queen took his hand in both of hers.

The Queen had already handed his medal to another United player and Norman Hunter helped Mick up to the Royal box.

Before his meeting with the Queen, Mick transferred his medal from one hand to the other.

He said later: "I was not going to miss that moment."

Pictured right: Jones attempts to go round Barnett in the run that brought tragedy.

Far right: Barnett and United trainer Les Cocker tend the injured Jones.

And the other hero . . .

What a goal!

A moment Leeds United fans will treasure is captured by the camera . . . Allan Clarke's superb goal which brought the F.A. Cup to Elland Road for the first time in the club's history.

With Arsenal skipper Frank McLintock (left) and his colleague Peter Simpson (No. 6) helpless bystanders as the ball flashes past the outstretched arms of 'keeper Geoff Barnett, United's captain Billy Bremner is on the spot to savour the shot which sent United's supporters roaring their appreciation.

Clarke's match-winning effort — which crowned an England-class performance by United's striker — came in the 53rd minute.

Jack Charlton began the move with a pass to winger Peter Lorimer, who flicked the ball to centre-forward Mick Jones on the right flank.

Jones tore past Huddersfield-born Bob McNab before centering for Clarke to beat the Arsenal 'keeper with a brilliant header.

The brilliantly-executed goal deserved to win the 100th F.A. Cup Final and earn its scorer the "Man of the match" award for the second time in his career.

The previous occasion Clarke was a member of the Leicester City side beaten by Manchester City in 1969. This time the story had a happy ending for the lethal six-footer.

A split second from victory. Allan Clarke's whip-crack header delivered from a full 16 yards zooms towards the Arsenal net. Geoff Barnett is airborne, arms outstretched, but, as Clarke said later, he did not have a chance. Peter Simpson is the defender on the left and Billy Bremner (inevitably) is near the action.

Scorer Allan Clarke and Mick Jones, who made the vital goal, share the precious moment.

The despair of Arsenal goalkeeper Geoff Barnett as Peter Simpson bends to pick the ball out of the net.

A picture taken from a different angle. Peter Lorimer was first to congratulate the jubilant Allan Clarke. But there is anguish on the face of Frank McLintock (left) and George Graham (right). In the background, Leeds fans stand to salute their heroes.

Yorkshire Evening Post special.

The TROPHY WINNERS

LEEDS UNITED
CENTENARY · F · A · CUP

THE F.A. CUP WAS FIRST WON IN 1872 .... AND JUST 100 YEARS LATER LEEDS UNITED CARRIED IT OFF FOR THE FIRST TIME IN THEIR HISTORY — AND IT WAS SUITABLE REWARD FOR SUCH CONSISTENT FORM IN RECENT YEARS....

THE YORKSHIRE TEAM BEGAN THEIR SUCCESSFUL CUP RUN LAST JANUARY, WITH AN EASY 4·1 WIN OVER THIRD DIVISION BRISTOL ROVERS.... **PETER LORIMER** (LEFT), WHO HITS A BALL AS HARD AS ANYONE IN THE GAME, FOUND THE NET TWICE IN THAT THIRD ROUND TIE. "LASH" LORIMER THUNDERED IN MORE THAN TWENTY SPECTACULAR GOALS FOR LEEDS — AND SCOTLAND — LAST SEASON....

NORMAN HUNTER AND **PAUL REANEY** TURN AWAY AS THE BALL IS IN THE SAFE HANDS OF **GARY SPRAKE**. GOALKEEPER SPRAKE LOST HIS PLACE IN THE TEAM — BUT WHO CAN DENY THAT ONLY A SUPERB SAVE BY HIM, AT LIVERPOOL, KEPT LEEDS IN THE CUP? LEEDS WON THE REPLAY....

ALLAN CLARKE ACCLAIMS A GOAL BY **MICK JONES** IN THE SEMI-FINAL. TWO BIRMINGHAM PLAYERS LOOK GLUM — AND LEEDS GO ON TO WIN 3·0....

JACK CHARLTON (RIGHT), PLAYED AS WELL AS EVER, AT 37 YEARS OF AGE. HE DIDN'T PUT A FOOT WRONG IN THE FINAL.... AND IT WAS BIG JACK'S BRILLIANT HEADER WHICH WON A HARD-FOUGHT SIXTH ROUND TIE WITH SPURS....

TWO GOALS FROM **JOHNNY GILES** (RIGHT), ENDED CARDIFF'S HOPES IN THE FIFTH ROUND AT NINIAN PARK....

Scorcher and Score Comic.

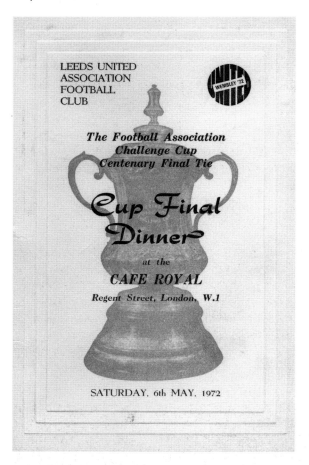

Don Revie's proud boast that Leeds United's team spirit is unrivalled is no empty claim. I shall remember 6 May 1972 as the day soccer star Allan Clarke unwittingly demonstrated that Leeds really is United.

Wembley Facts:
Goal Attempts: Leeds 17 (1 goal, 1 hit bar, 1 hit post, 3 saved, 2 deflected, 1 blocked, 8 wide or high) Arsenal 12 (1 hit bar, 4 saved, 1 deflected, 1 blocked, 5 wide or high)
Corners: Leeds 4 Arsenal 3
Fouls: Leeds 20 (including 2 handlings) Arsenal 24 (including 1 handling)
Bookings: Leeds 2 (Hunter, Bremner) Arsenal 2 (McNab, George)
Offsides: Leeds 4 Arsenal 1
Goal Kicks: Leeds 6 Arsenal 15
Substitutes: Leeds 0 Arsenal 1

The players enjoyed a hero's reception on the Wednesday evening, displaying the trophy on an open-top bus through the city centre before being greeted at Elland Road by a packed house.

Don Revie said:

'I just didn't believe it would be like this, these supporters make you feel very proud to belong to Leeds United. This has been a fantastic night, I did not expect so many people.'

Bremner added:

'This reception is overwhelming, I never thought we'd see a night like this, it was absolutely magnificent. I shall never forget it, I was very close to tears at times and so were some of the other players.'

Leeds United's triumphant team recall. David Harvey:

'I stayed in the side for the matches leading up to the final but never took my place for granted. It wasn't until the Thursday before the final that I was told I'd be playing. My initial feeling was one of disbelief. Even though I'd filled in for the previous games while Gary was injured and played okay, I fully expected to be told that he'd be back now he was fit. This had happened so many times before I took it for granted. When Gary was fit I was out, I accepted that. The rest of the side were told the next day. Don told us in no uncertain terms not to let ourselves down. He said: "If you're honest with yourself and play to the best of your ability you'll be fine. The easy way out is to bottle it, so don't." I'd been to Wembley before but this

was my first game as a player, my initial reaction was that the surface was just like a bowling green. I checked both goalmouths and remember thinking it was the lawn I'd always wanted. At this stage I wasn't nervous, maybe I should have been. When the game started, I was concentrating so hard I had no time to be affected by the glamour of the occasion. When we scored my first reaction was to keep calm, in any case I was too close to a heart attack to run up the field and congratulate everyone. I tapped my forehead and said to myself, touch wood, don't make a daft mistake, hang on for ten minutes and take the pressure out of the game. The most difficult time was the last fifteen minutes; it seemed to be going on forever. At the end of the game, I felt nothing more than sheer relief, and immediately celebrated with Norman and Jack. I felt great out there and really enjoyed it. Getting your medal and the lap of honour was tremendous, that's when my day started!'

Paul Reaney:

'We were always in control, but needed a break. When Allan scored, I knew we were not going to lose. As finals go, it went very quickly and was an unbelievable game to win because it was the centenary final. You think "savour the memories", and pick out certain things like Allan's goal and Alan Ball's shot that nearly went in, but you are concentrating so much on your game. The crowd hits you when you go out but when the game starts, even though there are 100,000 people there, you are concentrating on what you have to do and make sure you do it right. At the end, the feeling was joy more than relief. We'd done it, you had done your job, the gaffer, family and fans were happy. The only problem was we were not there to enjoy it afterwards for long, as we had to travel to Wolverhampton. It's impossible to place particular triumphs in order because they're all so special. The League Cup was personally memorable because it was our first major trophy, but naturally, after missing out twice before, the FA Cup was wonderful to finally win.'

Paul Madeley:

'It wasn't a classic final but throughout we were fairly solid and worthy winners. Allan scored a cracking goal and we only had a couple of anxious moments late on, especially when George hit the crossbar. The last ten minutes seemed to take an age. Collecting the medal and the lap of honour was fantastic, though they were over far too quickly. My overriding feeling was one of relief that we had finally won the FA Cup. There was added pressure going into the final because we did not want to be remembered as the team that always lost finals. In the dressing room afterwards, I gave Terry one of my stocking tags as my personal memento. There's something very special about Wembley on FA Cup final day that affects even the hardest of professional footballers. You remember how you watched the final as a kid, remember how it was always the biggest day of the football season, so it was a major ambition I'd set myself. When I was lucky enough to play in one and you hear that fantastic explosion of noise, and feel the butterflies as you walk out of the tunnel, you realise what people mean by Wembley magic. The centenary final is very special and it's a day I'll never forget. The win against Arsenal is my favourite one-off playing memory.'

Billy Bremner:

'We were a powerful outfit by then and Wembley isn't as daunting when you go back as an experienced team. In fact, we were more-or-less looking forward to the game. In my mind the only doubt I had was that we'd been in the FA Cup final twice before and lost both times. Would we win it this time? Maybe it put us under a bit more pressure because we knew here was an opportunity, are we going to get another? In saying that, we considered ourselves a little fortunate, after all many players only get one chance at Wembley and if it doesn't work out for them, that's hell. Whenever Leeds played Arsenal it was always a tight game, we always knew it was going to be hard. From the time Clarkie joined us in 1969 we didn't mind who we played, it may sound big-headed but that's far from it, we just felt comfortable wherever we went. We never thought we were going to lose a match no matter if it was Arsenal at Highbury, Manchester United at Old Trafford or Liverpool at Anfield. It didn't concern us, we never thought once about getting beaten. The gaffer was more nervous and concerned than any of the players. Every time I talked to him about the match he went on and on about Alan Ball's strengths and weaknesses, which I knew anyway because I played against him so many times. He believed that although Arsenal were better-organised since his transfer, his inclusion at the expense of Ray Kennedy slowed them down and reduced their counter-attacking options. I

always thought it was a tight game, however when I watched the highlights I couldn't believe how many times we broke on them in the last fifteen minutes. We had two on two and sometimes three on two, but guys were over elaborating when they had the chance to put someone else in. We should have won more convincingly. Also, I was amazed how much running Allan and Jonah did that day, they must have covered every blade of grass. After winning the FA Cup I felt we were a bit flat, maybe we should have had a few beers but we were worn out so just went to bed. In hindsight, we didn't particularly enjoy the victory long enough. People say to me, "you were in four FA Cup finals but you only won one". Well I say, "yeah but we won it". It is great just winning it the once, it doesn't matter that on three other occasions we missed out. Just to win it, to say we got our name down in the record books, it's enough.'

Jack Charlton:

'After all the agonies of last-fence failures he'd had to live through, I was delighted for Don Revie, but knowing Don he would have come up again next season if we had lost. He's was that kind of man. Two things stood out. I realised that it was probably my last chance of a winners' medal. In 1965 Don Revie told us not to be too down because we'd play in many more finals, in 1970 the final was just one game too far, so in 1972 I told myself this had to be third-time lucky. I was marking Charlie George and I remember thinking throughout whenever they came forward, "where's Charlie?" He was nowhere near me. Apart from one shot he caused us no problems at all.'

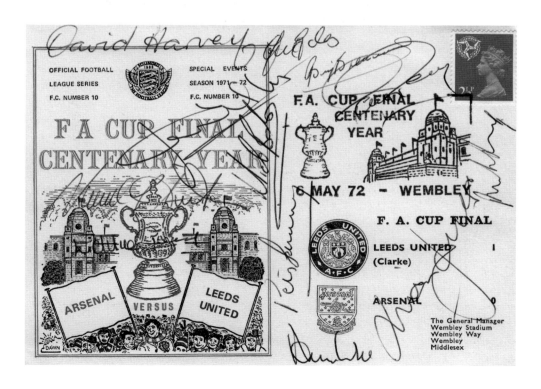

Norman Hunter:

'*At the end I was absolutely delighted because it was the first time we'd done it. You remember your losses more than your wins and when you get into the bath after losing its such an anticlimax. The losses stayed with me a damn sight longer. Winning is everything in this game. People forget you when you lose. I thought we won well.*'

Peter Lorimer:

'*We were motoring as a side and showing our true potential. Before the final, we had a good feeling about playing Arsenal as we had a good record against them. The match itself was played in a good spirit, although Bob McNab gave me a right kick in the first minute, but it looked worse than it was. From then on he was under pressure so I had a peaceful afternoon. The game passes by so quickly, I remember thinking, "bloody hell it's half-time already"; I could hardly believe it. In the end we won quite comfortably. Arsenal had a very good side but on the day we were the far better side. It was a lovely ball from Mick and they always say head it back across from the keeper. It was a great header by Allan.*'

Allan Clarke:

'*Walking up to get our medals was marvellous. Seeing Billy receive the FA Cup from the Queen and show it to our fans is something I'll never forget; it meant so much to him. The lap of honour itself was fantastic, it was one of those days when you didn't want to go into the dressing room, you just want to stay out on the pitch. Back in the changing rooms the FA Cup had been filled with champagne and we all drank from it the bath. The only sad sight was Jonah, who was resting on a bench in the corner before going to hospital; I sat with him for a while. We didn't go to the official banquet, our wives did. We went to the team coach and drove straight from Wembley with the FA Cup to the Mount Hotel near Wolverhampton. We all watched Match of the Day and were interviewed by the BBC. They say that you have to experience losing to appreciate the joy of winning. Well, after playing in two losing finals at the time I can honestly say winning is a whole lot better. Wembley is not a place for losers! There is something magic about the FA Cup. I played in four finals, lost three, but won the big one, the centenary FA Cup.'*

Mick Jones:

'Like all the lads, I couldn't wait for the final and we were determined not to slip up. Being involved with the winning goal is something I'll never forget but looking back I was sorry that I missed the final whistle, celebrations, going up for the cup and the lap of honour. Having said that, the reception the fans gave me as I was being carried off will always with live me. I'd achieved one of my greatest ambitions in winning the FA Cup and it was such a big ambition for us all. Also, to win the trophy in the competition's centenary year was superb.'

Johnny Giles:

'I won the trophy in 1963, which was special because it was a new experience, but 1972 was different, it meant an awful lot to me because of the team spirit. When I joined Leeds most of the 1972 team were already at the club, though only Billy and Jack were experienced. We all grew up together and became a great team by the late 1960s and with the likes of Terry Cooper, Paul Madeley, Peter Lorimer and Eddie Gray we matured and played some wonderful stuff. Between 1968 and 1972 we were the best side in the country, in fact from Christmas to the FA Cup final, we peaked, playing football that I have never seen bettered anywhere and I would say you are unlikely to see again. When I looked around our dressing room I knew that we had a team that could not only battle but also play.'

Eddie Gray:

'We played quite well that day, it was a tight match but throughout we were comfortable, and Allan scored a great goal. The only disappointment was Mick injuring himself so badly. Looking back, it means so much because we lost other finals. For me it was certainly one of my best playing memories.'

Mick Bates:

'We were all nervous on the bench. Watching is never easy but you get used to it. The longer it went on the more nerve-wracking it became, even though we were in control and a goal up. At the final whistle the relief was incredible, I remember leaping off the bench and hugging everybody. When I went up with the team for our medals the Queen gave me two. I must be the only person to receive two medals for a game in which I never had a kick!'

142

11

Double Disaster

With little time to prepare for a clash that would decide the destiny of the league championship and double, Revie surveyed his walking wounded. Definitely out at Wolves was Mick Jones and, on a night of unbearable tension, Allan Clarke, Johnny Giles and Eddie Gray played with injuries that would have seen them rested under normal circumstances. Leeds battled away and but for appalling refereeing would have won. Twice Wolves full-back Bernard Shaw handled, but neither the referee or linesman saw an infringement. Wolves' opening goal just before half-time was deflected by two players, and when Derek Dougan blasted home a second all seemed over. However, Bremner gave Leeds hope when he converted Madeley's cross, and almost snatched a draw in the last minute, but Gerry Taylor cleared his backward header off the line. In defeat though, there was nothing but praise from the Leeds boss and national media. Don Revie said:

'I thought we should have had three clear penalties. It was definitely handball twice. It's just too much. When you get decisions like that going against you, what can you do? But I was proud of the team even in defeat. I don't know where they got the energy from in the second half.'

Alan Thompson (*Daily Express*):

Leeds failed by twenty-three minutes to complete a magnificent double last night, and a weary and dispirited side walked off the Molineux pitch after having fought to their last drop of energy. They beat the teams on the way but they couldn't beat the fixture planners and they couldn't beat either Wolverhampton or ill-luck that has dogged them all season, but though the record books will never show it, they are for me the FA Cup winners AND league champions.

Eric Todd (*The Guardian*):

This surely will go down as one of the bravest failures of all time. Indeed, I would hesitate to call it a failure at all. As if to cock a snook at authority, which demanded they should play a league game during cup final week and another one two days after Wembley, Leeds gave of their considerable best. And if Bremner has played a more inspiring game I wish I had seen it.

WOLVES
71-72

OFFICIAL
MATCH-DAY
MAGAZINE
Vol. 4 No. 28

U.E.F.A. CUP GOAL JOY — SEE PAGE 23

Molineux, Monday, 8th May, 1972   Kick-off 7.30 p.m.

WOLVES v LEEDS UNITED

It's not to be... the double dream dies at Molineux.

Don Warters (*Evening Post*):

If ever a team had cause to feel bitter, United have today. Leeds should have received three penalties. For the players it must have felt like knives being driven slowly into their backs.

Bobby Charlton (*Goal*):

Leeds haven't always been a side to earn the sympathy of the public down the years but what happened to them in the final run-in was pretty diabolical. Being forced to play the all-important league game only two days after winning the FA Cup at Wembley was a bit off. Sometimes I wonder whether the people who make these decisions know what it is like to play in a cup final. It ties your stomach in knots and exhausts you so much, both mentally and physically, that it is just about impossible to completely recover 100 per cent in forty-eight hours. Leeds of course had to abide by the decision to play Wolves on the following Monday but then what happens? They were fighting well, the score was still 0-0 and then they get the best-looking penalty I've seen in years. The TV cameras clearly showed a Wolves defender handling the ball in the box but all Leeds' claims were turned down. If it had been awarded, as it should have been, the whole course of the Championship would have been changed and Leeds would almost certainly added their name to those of Spurs and Arsenal as historic double winners. It was not to be and they had to settle for the cup instead.

Looking back, Allan Clarke says:

'There's no doubt in my mind that the FA's insistence the game take place so close to the FA Cup final affected us. In the dressing room afterwards, you'd have thought you were at a funeral. The aftermath of the pitch invasion against West Brom caught up with us. If we had played all our games at Elland Road the title would have been wrapped up before the final. But no one could take away the feeling we had immediately after winning the FA Cup that season, it was unbelievable.'

Paul Reaney added:

'Wolves was a great disappointment. It was a shame we were forced to play on the Monday having played at Wembley. They had nothing to play for, which was maybe to their advantage. We only needed a draw and were so disappointed after that game you would not have thought we'd won the FA Cup forty-eight hours before. The gaffer was saying "come on, you're FA Cup winners", but we were league losers and that was devastating. I should have cleared off the line for their first goal but David Harvey dived in front of me and just touched the ball, and it went in. If he had not been there, who knows what the result would have been because I would have stopped it? Although fatigue was there we knew what we wanted but just could not get it. The season was still a success. We won the FA Cup and got to the last game to claim the double. Some teams finish in the top four and think they have had a fantastic year. We won the cup and came runners-up by a point. That's not failure; it's all about expectations.'

FA Cup winners. Back: Reaney, Charlton, Harvey, Jones, Hunter, Madeley. Front: Lorimer, Clarke, Bremner, Giles, Bates, Gray.

Watching on from the sidelines, Mick Jones recalls:

'Doc Adams collected me from my house, I have never seen so much traffic; it was chock-a-block all the way to Birmingham. When we got to the ground, thousands were locked out. I eventually got in and went to see the lads in the dressing room. I couldn't get a seat for the game, so stood in a little press box behind the goal. Watching was worse than playing, because you could see we weren't going to do it, even though the lads gave everything. If the game had been played a couple of days later, we'd have clinched the double, I'm convinced of that. It is hard enough playing against teams when we had time to prepare, but to have only forty-eight hours to recover from the cup final was so unjust.'

The double ultimately eluded Leeds United but the memories never fade away. It was a season that encapsulated an amazing decade when Revie's Leeds dominated English football. Of course, there is no doubt they could have claimed more honours, but you won't find recriminations from the players because they know they were part of something very special. Billy Bremner sums up a golden era:

'People say to me we should have won more. Yeah, that's true. In reality, however, we had a fantastic record. We were always involved right to the death and most players would have given their right arm to be in our position every year. For a ten-year period, everybody wanted to beat us.

I just loved playing. I used to think, "I'm lucky I can play a game that I get paid for, that I would do for nothing." The biggest thing for me was to be able to play with a bunch of guys that got on well with each other over the long period of time we were together. With the exception of Allan, Johnny and Mick, who we bought as young men, we were all Leeds boys and that principally generated the team's family spirit. We only knew Leeds United and we loved Leeds United.

Many of us had never heard of the club before we came, so to grow up and love that club was tremendous. The biggest thrill I ever had was wearing the white shirt of Leeds United. Other teams like Liverpool and Manchester United had great traditions. Without being disrespectful to the teams that preceded us, our club never achieved any major success before Don arrived. Yes, there were great individual players before us but our team set the standards and targets that future Leeds teams are compared with and try to emulate. It was a wonderful time.'

A Personal View
by Billy Bremner

Who better to talk about the Boys of '72 than the skipper himself? In an interview in 1997, Billy spoke about his teammates from the FA Cup final triumph.

'David Harvey was superb in the final, especially when you consider it was not long before that he had won his place for the semi-final. He was a very accomplished goalkeeper, not flash, kept good angles, had great hands and was a very conscientious trainer. David was a nice steadying influence for the boys.

Paul Reaney was always going to be steady. He was not particularly gifted as a passer but he was a brilliant defender. They talk about players having pace nowadays but Paul was exceptionally quick. Not only was he quick but also if he was sold a dummy and happened to go on his backside I've never seen anyone get back up and challenge again. He was an outstanding defender.

Some people remember Paul Madeley as a substitute... such a substitute. He played more games for Leeds United than virtually any other player! He was always in the side, whether he was left-back, right-back, centre-back, midfield or up front, he always played. Though he was big, Paul was never a physical player or vindictive. I'd say to him sometimes "Get into him, get a few in." Paul would say "Why?" Paul was silky, like a Rolls Royce when on a football pitch. Also, he was a nice passer of the ball and deceptively quick too. He used to move at a steady pace and then, with what appeared to be no effort whatsoever, went into a higher gear before pulling away. Paul was a stalwart for us.

My opinion of Jack Charlton is not just because he was my roommate, it's the confidence I had in him. No matter where we went, if I had Jack with me as centre half I thought we could take on the world. I knew there were not many people who would beat the 'Big Man' in the air, or outrun the 'Big Man', because the 'Big Man' was bloody quick. Yet with those big legs of his he could make great tackles, though he did make those crazy runs forward. He kept thinking he was a centre forward!

Alongside Big Jack was his sidekick, Norman Hunter. Norman was a tremendous professional and few bettered him. He was very unfortunate that he was vying for the same England position as Bobby Moore. Without Bobby, many more caps would undoubtedly have come Norman's way. Norman was hard, but he wasn't just hard, you don't play at that level of football unless you had skill. Norman read games and people's reactions exceptionally well and could nip in front of people when balls were being nicked into their feet. When he had the ball himself, Norman was a great passer, he could hit them long, short, was good in the air, and his timing was excellent. I thought Norman was a marvellous player, I really did.

Peter Lorimer scored goals that no-one else could. Most free-kicks in range Peter would say, "I'll hit it" so we'd move away. He was an enigma, you couldn't tell him what to do on a football pitch, generally he'd do his own thing. Peter had a lot more skill than people gave him credit for, he really did. He was such an accurate passer of the ball and had a great belief in himself. I've never known a football player with such a belief in his own ability to do well. Even when he wasn't doing well he still thought he was!

Allan Clarke was a good passer of the ball and had great control. He was also incredibly calm in front of goal and rarely missed a one-on-one opportunity, a clinical finisher. Being able to score with both head and feet, Allan was invaluable to the side, and from the time he joined gave us more attacking options than we ever had. Clarke and Jonah blended extremely well together.

Mick Jones was the opposite to Clarkie, he was the target man and the warhorse. Mick went after this ball, he went after that ball and he chased any lost cause. Even though Mick knew a ball was going out of play he would still go after it just in case an opportunity developed. People would get frustrated with him, they'd think, "not this bugger again". The beauty about Mick was that he rarely reacted to anything, he just picked himself up and walked away. I used to think to myself, "how do you do that?" But Mick could, he had a great temperament.

Johnny Giles and myself complemented each other. I would have loved the job that Johnny did, but because he was so accomplished at it, I was unable to. He'd go back for the ball and pick it up and distribute it. My job was to support the forwards. Johnny was such a calming influence on me if things weren't going well. Apart from complementing each other, both of us could look after ourselves for two short guys! There were a lot of players who would love to have "given us one" in the middle of a game. We didn't work on our style of play. People used to say it was telepathic the way the two of us linked, we just seemed to blend well together.

We had a genius at outside left. If Eddie Gray hadn't suffered the injuries that he did he would have become one of the truly great players of world football, I really do believe that. Eddie was a fantastic player, there were no attributes in the game he didn't have. Eddie could go past you on your left or right side; he would go past people for fun. Eddie could take it with his left, he could take it with his right and came at you side on. He could bend balls and could hit them with the outside or inside of his foot. Also, when Eddie went past people he immediately had his head up to pick colleagues out. I've never seen a boy do so many tricks with a ball as Eddie could. The only wee flaw he had, and it wasn't a conscious thing, was that I believe he should have scored more goals. The thing that surprised people with Eddie was his height, they never realised how big he was. Eddie was a tremendous athlete and a great player.

Mick Bates was a good wee player, he used to come in and do extremely well when either Johnny or I was injured. Mick was smashing because he played the game the way we all played it. He didn't try anything elaborate in midfield, he got it and he passed it, he went for returns, he got forward when he had to get forward. He was also a nice fella. People used to ask me why he didn't leave Leeds and maybe play in someone else's first team. The simple answer was that he was happy at the club.'

As for Billy, his teammates offered these tributes. Norman Hunter:

'Billy was a great player. In my opinion you will never get a better combination than Giles and Bremner. He was a good skipper, but you had a lot of captains out there that took charge, talking to you and sorting it out in their own way. Billy also scored some vital goals. During a game if we needed a goal the gaffer used to jump up with ten minutes or quarter of an hour to go. He'd shout, 'Billy, sort yourselves out', and we let him go. Don looked at us all and we complemented each other. We all did certain things. They scored goals; we defended. We were very much together as a team and if Billy was good at scoring, Don would think, "go on get up there".'

Paul Madeley:

'Billy was some player and everything people thought; tenacious, good on the ball and he had a great attitude. He was such an inspiration and a true leader in every sense of the word. He could never have been just an also ran, no matter who he played for. To me his main strength as captain was his ability to motivate. If you did something good on the pitch, he'd be there saying, "that's terrific", and if you made a mess of it he wouldn't say anything in case you lost confidence. Billy had such an influence on the side with his incredible will to win stamped all over him. Of course, he had a fiery temperament, but he was so competitive and desperate to win every game. I've never known anyone with such a fierce determination to succeed. Billy was also so naturally fit. Whenever he came back from injury, which was not that often, it didn't take him long to regain fitness. He just slotted straight back in, charging about, getting tackles in and causing havoc for opponents. In midfield, Billy made great runs to create opportunities for goals, whereas Johnny Giles concentrated on defence-splitting passes; they were the perfect partnership. Billy also scored many important goals in crucial matches. He was an incredible player; the greatest I played with in my career.'

Peter Lorimer:

'I've never seen a player whose fitness in general was poor pre-season but could then expend so much energy in a football match in a season for ninety minutes and never look tired. If Billy went on a run, he wouldn't get to the end of the block. He used to say, "it's not about running it's about how you play football", and that's how he played football; he was an amazing character. Billy had this belief in himself that only he could get us out of trouble. When we got behind his feeling was, "I'll sort it". Gilesy would say, "he's gone", and pull us in a bit. Then Billy would score a goal and be the hero!'

Allan Clarke:

'Billy was the best player I ever played with. Billy loved being skipper of Leeds and Scotland and had it all; fitness, speed, guts and style. He was a ball-winner one moment, a goalscorer the next. Billy was at times temperamental, but that was his nature; he was a winner. Although he played in midfield, the ground he covered was phenomenal. His determination and enthusiasm was exceptional and many of his goals were crucial. Billy played many games

when unfit but was so inspirational he couldn't and wouldn't be left out. Billy is the most famous player to pull on the white shirt of Leeds United.'

Paul Reaney:

'Before signing for Leeds I saw Billy playing from the terraces when he was a right-winger, Don was still playing. Then all of a sudden I was chucked in and I'm training with him. He was a great captain on and off the pitch. Billy would give you as much stick as Don, and played the game in training as in a match; the Scotland v. England clashes were always a bit tasty! I had to mark him and it was not an easy job because he so wanted to win. You could go on and on about Billy. He was great technician, passer and could score goals. Billy could do anything he wanted to do. As with all the lads, I'd rather play with him than against him.'

Mick Jones:

'Billy was a winner, simple as that. He was determined, enthusiastic and a battler. Billy also scored so many important goals for a midfield player. Billy had so much ability, many a time he joined the attack with devastating effect; he could have played anywhere. Billy may have been temperamental but that was because of his will to win; he was undoubtedly a world-class footballer. Billy Bremner was the dressing room; he was at the centre of everything both on and off the pitch.'

Super Leeds

Don Revie utilised twenty-three players throughout the 1971/72 campaign. Detailed here are biographies of every player that made at least 10 appearances during the season, in addition to manager Revie. Norman Hunter, Peter Lorimer and Paul Madeley were ever-present in the League campaign, Billy Bremner and Jack Charlton missed just one match. Lorimer top scored with 23 goals. In the FA Cup, Bremner, Hunter, Lorimer, Madeley and Johnny Giles played in every tie; Allan Clarke and Giles top scored with 4 goals apiece. Lorimer top scored in all competitions with 29 goals. Players not detailed in the following biopics are Nigel Davey, Keith Edwards, John Faulker, Chris Galvin, Jimmy Mann and John Shaw.

DON REVIE

DON REVIE is a name synonymous with Leeds United. Manager during the club's glory years, Revie converted a team heading for obscurity into one of European football's most feared outfits. Every Leeds manager since has faced comparison, which, while understandable, is grossly unfair because the squad that Revie built was a one-off. Appearance-wise, the club's top-ten is filled with Revie's players and the standard of consistency set by his team for a decade will never be equalled.

Born in Middlesbrough, 10 July 1927, Revie began his playing career in 1944 at Leicester City before a £20,000 fee took him to Hull City in 1949. A cultured inside right, within two years Manchester City paid £25,000 for his services. At Maine

Road, Revie made his name as a deep-lying centre forward, his distribution skills suiting a system dubbed the 'Revie plan'. His performances earned him the Football Writers' Player of the Year award in 1954/55. Though City lost the FA Cup final to Newcastle United, Revie starred in his side's 3-1 win over Birmingham City twelve months later. Within eighteen months Revie was a Sunderland player following a £22,000 transfer before he ended his playing days at Leeds United after a £12,000 move.

Following his debut in a 3-2 win against Newcastle United, Revie was appointed captain, before passing the honour to Freddie Goodwin after a number of bad results. Playing twice for the Football League Representative XI, on the international stage Revie was unfortunate to win only 6 caps for England. It would be as a manager, however, that he would receive international acclaim, but his entry to the profession had a large slice of luck to begin with. Nearing the end of the 1960/61 season thirty-three-year-old Revie applied for the manager's post at Bournemouth. Needing a reference, he asked Leeds director Harry Reynolds to oblige but, while penning the letter, Reynolds realised that Revie was the person Leeds United needed despite his lack of managerial experience. His fellow directors agreed to give Revie a chance and the greatest period in the club's history began. Initially player-manager, Revie insisted on the best travel and conditions for his players, changed the club strip to the all-white of Real Madrid and began the process of developing the best youth policy in the country. Following his retirement as a player, towards the end of his debut season at the helm in 1961/62, Leeds were bottom with eleven games left. In need of an experienced campaigner, Revie turned to Bobby Collins. The Leeds boss's hunch worked to perfection as Collins inspired his charges to safety in the final game at Newcastle United. The following term Revie introduced some of his talented youngsters alongside Collins, Jack Charlton, Billy Bremner, Willie Bell and Albert Johanneson. Displaying undoubted potential, Gary Sprake, Paul Reaney and Norman Hunter showed their worth in the first team.

Johnny Giles and Alan Peacock's arrival in 1963/64 helped secure the Second Division title and the double was tantalisingly close the following term as Leeds finished runners-up in both League and FA Cup. The next three seasons would see the likes of Terry Cooper, Paul Madeley and Peter Lorimer strengthen the team as Leeds continued to go close to honours, finishing runners-up in the First Division and the Fairs Cup, in addition to reaching the semi-finals of the Fairs Cup and FA Cup.

Leeds' pursuit of honours brought accusations of a 'win-at-all-costs' mentality. Some games were brutal and Revie's players did contest refereeing decisions, hustled opponents and were over-zealous at times, but to be dubbed 'dirty Leeds' by the media, a tag that stuck for years, was outrageous.

Tactically astute, Revie's attention to detail was legendary. Producing detailed dossiers on opponents, Revie left nothing to chance. A superb organiser and spotter of talent, Revie's greatest strength was his man-management skill. Requiring a big squad to battle on all fronts, while the likes of Sprake, Reaney, Cooper, Hunter, Lorimer and Gray were stalwarts of the side, others such as Mick Bates, David

Harvey, Rod Belfitt, Jimmy Greenhoff and Terry Hibbitt were also essential. Good enough to play regularly in the First Division, as a number eventually did, each player made significant contributions during the development of the side in the mid-1960s. Balancing the needs of a squad packed with international stars was no easy task, but Revie received absolute loyalty from his players.

At the start of the 1967/68 campaign, Revie strengthened his side by signing Mick Jones. Leeds finally won a major trophy when Terry Cooper's strike against Arsenal secured the League Cup, and Jones grabbed the only goal of the Fairs Cup final against Ferencvaros of Hungary to secure the club's first European trophy. Revie's team was now unstoppable and, after five years' endeavour, finally claimed the most coveted domestic prize, the First Division championship trophy in 1968/69, with a record number of points. Revie won the prestigious Manager of the Year award and, with the addition of Allan Clarke prior to the start of the 1969/70 season, Leeds now had the most clinical strike force around.

At the dawn of a new decade, Revie began to remove the defensive restraints on his team and Leeds finally received the plaudits their talents deserved. Securing the Fairs Cup in 1970/71, Revie's boys hit a peak during the second half of the 1971/72 campaign, when their football at times was simply breathtaking. Inventive, resourceful and dazzling, no Leeds supporter will ever forget an awesome display as Manchester United were swept aside 5-1, but the performance that summed up Revie's team's capabilities came in the dying moments of the 7-0 annihilation of Southampton when they kept their opponents at bay with a display of keep-ball. Sniffer Clarke's diving header finally secured the FA Cup that term and, with David Harvey, Trevor Cherry, Joe Jordan, Gordan McQueen and Terry Yorath becoming regulars, Leeds claimed a second First Division title in 1973/74, a season when they went twenty-nine games undefeated from the start of the campaign.

Although Leeds won six major trophies, more than any other team from 1968 to 1974, they should have claimed more. First Division runners-up five times, FA Cup runners-up on three occasions and losing finalists in the Fairs Cup and European Cup Winners' Cup, their most trying season came in 1969/70 when only fatigue and fixture congestion denied them a League, FA Cup and European Cup treble. Nevertheless, Revie's boys always finished in the top four of the First Division and was the team to beat every season. Playing to packed houses, they were the most talked-about and written-about club in domestic football. Revie's side is the greatest in the club's history and his team set standards that others have to attempt to match. It had been an incredible journey for Revie and his team but it was time for the greatest manager in the club's history to move on after a glorious decade of success.

Revie accepted the challenge of managing England in July 1974 but, despite capping many players, found it impossible to recreate the 'club' atmosphere at international level. After initially improving results, when qualification to the 1978 World Cup was out of reach, Revie accepted a lucrative job to coach the United Arab Emirates, amid rumours of his imminent sacking by the Football Association. Announcing his decision in the *Daily Mail* before informing FA officials, Revie was heavily criticised by his former employers and the media. The FA imposed a ban on

Revie from working in England, which Revie successfully overturned, but the former England manager's reputation never recovered nationally. Apart from a consulting role at Leeds, Revie never managed another league club.

When Don Revie died in May 1989 of motor neurone disease, the city of Leeds mourned. The greatest manager in the club's history, Revie, awarded the OBE in 1970, put Leeds United on the football map worldwide and made household names of his star players. One can always speculate how many trophies Leeds may have claimed if Revie had let his team off the leash earlier or brought the more reliable Harvey in for Sprake sooner than he did. However, despite being excessively superstitious and over-estimating opponents his team was more than capable of defeating comfortably at times, nobody should be too critical of Revie because no manager since at Elland Road has come close to matching his achievements. Three decades on, Revie's legendary side is acknowledged as one of the greatest ever post-war teams and memories of his outstanding team live on in numerous videos and DVDs. However, the true test of what this remarkable manager achieved is to speak to football supporters around the globe. Wherever you go, all can name player by player the great Leeds United side that Revie built. That is Don Revie's legacy.

MICK BATES

MICK BATES was not an automatic first choice for Leeds United's first team during his twelve-year association with the club but he fulfilled an essential role in Don Revie's legendary squad as they took on all-comers at home and abroad. Born in Doncaster, 19 September 1947, after playing for Yorkshire Schools, Bates joined Leeds as an apprentice, signing professional forms in 1964. The Under-18 side was packed with talent, when you consider his teammates included the likes of David Harvey, Peter Lorimer and Eddie Gray. With so much competition for places, patience was essential and Bates needed to have it because he had to wait until 1965/66 to make his first-team debut against Hartlepool in the League Cup.

Making 12 appearances the following term, it could not have been easy watching from the sidelines for long periods but it did not help that he had to compete with Billy Bremner and Johnny Giles for a midfield berth. Nevertheless, whenever called upon, Bates, modest, compact and a fine passer of the ball, never let anyone down and was a valuable member of Revie's legendary squad.

Bates's role, like Rod Belfitt, Jimmy Greenhoff, Terry Hibbitt and eventually Terry Yorath, was a testament to Revie's man-management skills because all could undoubtedly have been a regular for the majority of First Division teams. Revie, however, realised the importance of a big pool of players with his team battling on all fronts, and a player of Bates's calibre and loyalty was a vital element to his overall strategy. All stayed at least five years, Bates the longest, and would win more honours.

During his years at Leeds, Bates enjoyed extended first-team runs in 1970/71 and 1972/73, and his 10 league appearances in 1973/74, scoring the only goal at Manchester City and netting a sweet strike against West Ham, proved significant during a key stage of the championship-winning campaign. A member of both Fairs Cup winning sides, the highlight of his career came in the first leg of the 1970/71 final against Juventus when he scored a cracking equaliser in the 2-2 draw in Turin, which proved decisive as Leeds won the trophy on away goals. A non-playing substitute in two FA Cup finals, Bates's last appearance in a major final ended in heartbreak after Leeds' infamous European Cup Winners' Cup defeat to AC Milan in 1973.

At the end of the 1975/76 season Bates joined Walsall for £25,000, where he skippered the side during a two-year spell. In 1978, he joined Bradford City for £20,000 before playing briefly for Doncaster Rovers. Mick Bates may not have grabbed the headlines like many of his famous colleagues but his 187 appearances for Leeds were crucial and recognised by his colleagues and supporters alike during a glorious decade of success at Elland Road.

ROD BELFITT

ROD BELFITT was unable to command a regular place in Leeds United's first team throughout his eight years with the club. Nevertheless, he fulfilled an important role in Don Revie's legendary squad. Born in Doncaster, 30 October 1945, Belfitt played for Doncaster United and Retford Town, while training as a draughtsman, before joining Leeds as an apprentice in July 1963. A member of a fine Under-18 side that included the likes of David Harvey, Peter Lorimer and Eddie Gray, Belfitt was one of the first youngsters to break through to the first team as a replacement for Don Weston against Blackpool in September 1964. Belfitt's first goal followed swiftly with the winner in a 3-2 League Cup victory against

Huddersfield Town. Playing 9 games during the 1964/65 campaign, Belfitt scored an impressive 5 goals. Over the coming seasons though, with the arrival of Mick Jones in 1967 and Allan Clarke in 1970, Belfitt would rarely feature in First Division fixtures, starting 10 games in 1966/67 and 1971/72, and 11 in 1967/68.

Cup competitions, however, would enable Belfitt to make his mark. After a European bow against Valencia in 1965/66, Belfitt featured prominently in the following term's Fairs Cup, notching his only Leeds hat-trick in a 4-2 aggregate win against Kilmarnock in the semi-finals. Reaching a first European final was a major triumph for Leeds despite a 2-0 defeat. Belfitt played in both legs against Dynamo Zagreb. In 1967/68, after a number of near-misses, honours finally came to Elland Road. Belfitt missed only one tie in Leeds' march to the League Cup final, coming up trumps in the semi-final second leg against Derby County. Belfitt's brace ensured Leeds reached Wembley 4-3 on aggregate. Unlucky not to start the final against Arsenal, Belfitt made his only appearance at the Twin Towers as a second-half substitute for Gray. During four Fairs Cup appearances, Belfitt struck a crucial goal in a 3-2 win over Partizan Belgrade and came on as a substitute for Jones in the first leg of the final against Ferencvaros.

Belfitt's reliability was a tribute to his manager's man-management skills. Revie knew the importance of a big squad and Belfitt's calibre and loyalty was vital to his overall strategy. Although not dangerous aerially like Jones, Belfitt shielded the ball well, had a neat touch and his 33 goals proved important. In 8 league games during 1968/69, Belfiit scored 3 times, but all were in tight matches and gained valuable points in two hard-fought victories against Ipswich Town and a draw against Sunderland.

In November 1971, Belfitt decided to join Ipswich. Staying one year, he also played briefly for Everton, Sunderland, Fulham and Huddersfield Town prior to winding down his career at a number of non-league clubs. A fringe player maybe, Belfitt appeared 128 times for Leeds United, but his task was essential during the Revie era. A member of the squads that won the League Cup and Fairs Cup, Rod Belfitt was a fine player for the club.

BILLY BREMNER

BILLY BREMNER is the greatest player ever to represent Leeds United. His never-say-die attitude, playing ability and inspirational leadership drove the team forward throughout the Don Revie era; taking the club from Second Division minnows to one of European football's most respected and feared outfits.

Born in Stirling on 9 December 1942, Bremner was considered too small by Arsenal and Chelsea. Joining Leeds at seventeen, he made his debut in January 1960 against Chelsea. One of his teammates was Don Revie before his appointment as manager. Despite early setbacks due to homesickness, his playing career at Elland Road would span sixteen years.

Revie recognised the raw talent Bremner possessed, even though his fiery temperament resulted in a number of brushes with the Football Association. Throughout Bremner's career his desire to win never diminished. A classic picture with Dave Mackay summed up his attitude following an incident at White Hart Lane in the mid-1960s. Mackay does not look amused following the clash!

Playing alongside future skipper Bobby Collins and Jack Charlton in 1961/62, Leeds escaped relegation when Third Division football seemed inevitable and, with the introduction of youngsters such as Gary Sprake, Paul Reaney and Norman Hunter, Leeds improved rapidly, clinching the Second Division title in 1963/64; their first divisional success for forty years. Taking the First Division by storm, Leeds astounded everyone by finishing runners-up in both the league and FA Cup. Though heartbreaking, supporters will never forget Bremner's winner in the dying minutes of the cup semi-final against Manchester United and even though Liverpool edged the Wembley final, Bremner scored a scorcher as an exciting era dawned.

The 1965/66 campaign saw Bremner appointed captain following a long-term injury to Collins in a Fairs Cup clash and, under his leadership, Leeds claimed the First Division title and Fairs Cup twice, FA Cup, League Cup and Charity Shield. In addition, Revie's team finished First Division runners-up five times, lost three FA Cup finals and two European finals. Bremner missed the European Cup Winners' Cup final defeat due to suspension. Although many honours eluded Leeds, the team's consistency was unrivalled for a decade.

One of the most recognised footballers of his era, Bremner was voted Footballer of the Year in 1969/70. Having represented Scotland at Schoolboy and Under-23 level, he made his full Scottish debut against Spain in 1965. Acknowledged as world class, Bremner faced all the legendary players of world football. Winning 54 caps, many as captain, Bremner's finest moment came when he led Scotland in the 1974 World Cup finals. Arguably, however, the most famous game he played for his country was when Scotland defeated England 3-2 at Wembley to become the first team to defeat the 1966 World Cup winners.

As a player he had everything – strength, stamina, fine passing and shooting ability, and brilliant anticipation. Bremner was a ball-winner one moment, a goalscorer the next. At times for Leeds he also excelled as an emergency defender, striker or sweeper but it was in midfield, in tandem with Johnny Giles, that he made his mark. Bremner and Giles complemented each other perfectly, becoming the most feared midfield partnership at home and in Europe.

For a midfield player, Bremner's haul of 115 goals was an incredible achievement and many of them were crucial. Three in FA Cup semi-finals took Leeds to Wembley and his flying header at Liverpool won a classic Fairs Cup semi-final clash in 1971. On five occasions Bremner hit double figures during a season. The last in 1973/74 was particularly special, as many pundits had written Revie's team off following the cup final disappointments the previous season. As an unbeaten run of 29 games engineered a second championship, the diminutive Scot scored 10 goals, including two in the run-in against Derby and Ipswich, which proved vital.

Following Don Revie's departure to become England manager it was only a matter of time before Bremner moved on. There would be one more Wembley appearance in the Charity Shield when he was sensationally sent off for fighting Kevin Keegan, before a final tilt at the European Cup. During a memorable campaign, Bremner scored a tremendous goal against Barcelona in the semi-final, before the ultimate prize was snatched from his grasp in the final after some dubious refereeing decisions. Bremner made his last appearance for Leeds at Elland Road in a 2-2 with Newcastle United in September 1976, taking his total number of appearances for the club to 773, a record he shares with Jack Charlton, before joining Hull City for £35,000. His transfer was a major coup for the Tigers and helped swell attendances but he wanted to become a manager and got his chance with Doncaster Rovers in 1978. After a handful of games, he finally retired as a player and guided Rovers twice to promotion. In October 1985, he replaced Eddie Gray at his beloved Leeds United.

Languishing in the Second Division, despite limited funds, Bremner threw himself into the job and by the start of the 1986/87 season had rebuilt the team around Mervyn Day, John Sheridan and Ian Baird. With self-belief among his players increasing throughout a memorable campaign, his endeavours to guide Leeds back into the big time appeared on track as Leeds battled to the semi-finals of the FA Cup and the Second Division play-off final. Heartbreakingly, Leeds failed when success appeared within reach, losing to Coventry City in a memerorable semi-final and, even more dramatically, Charlton Athletic overturned a Sheridan strike in the last seven minutes to deny a return to top-flight football. It was a crushing end to a pulsating campaign.

After the dust had settled Bremner's reward was an extended contract but the players failed to deliver in 1987/88 and, after making a poor start the following term, his association with Leeds United ended. Bremner's tenure may have finished but his presence had brought renewed hope for long-suffering supporters. Following a two-year spell with Doncaster Rovers, Bremner began a career as an accomplished after-dinner speaker until his sudden death in 1997, aged fifty-four.

Today, a statue of Billy Bremner greets supporters to Elland Road, a reminder of the fighting spirit he displayed endlessly for the club. King Billy is the most successful captain in Leeds United's history. A legend, his achievements will never be forgotten.

JACK CHARLTON

JACK CHARLTON is one of Leeds United's greatest ever servants. Big Jack was a member of a remarkable footballing family. Elder brother to Manchester United and England legend Bobby, three of his uncles, George, Jim and Jack Milburn, all served Leeds with distinction. Indeed, Jim recommended his nephew while he was playing at Elland Road.

Born in Ashington, 8 May 1935, Charlton joined Leeds as an amateur in 1950 before signing professional forms in 1952. Following his debut against Doncaster Rovers on the last day of the 1952/53 season, the lanky defender had to wait until the 1955/56 campaign to receive an extended run in the first team. Raich Carter was manager and, with Leeds struggling for goals, Carter switched John Charles to centre forward and brought the inexperienced Charlton in at centre half.

Few pundits backed Leeds for promotion due to their inconsistency but eight wins in their last nine games snatched the runners-up spot behind Sheffield Wednesday. It had been mighty close though and, but for a 4-1 victory at Hull City in the last game of the season, Leeds would have missed out.

Charlton's progress earned the first of six appearances for the Football League in 1957. However, with John Charles now at Juventus, playing in a struggling side hindered his development. It didn't help matters that his stubborn nature and strongly held views made for an uneasy relationship with management. Nevertheless new boss Don Revie believed in his ability and began to get the best out of him. Astonishingly, Charlton filled in as an emergency centre forward for a couple of seasons as Revie grappled with an injury crisis among his strikers and he never let his boss down, top scoring alongside Billy Bremner in 1961/62 as relegation to the Third Division was just averted! Centre of defence though was where Charlton would make his name.

With the introduction of Bobby Collins and youngsters Gary Sprake, Paul Reaney and Norman Hunter, Leeds improved rapidly, clinching the Second Division title in 1963/64; their first divisional success for forty years. A key member of the side, Charlton's performances the following term, when Leeds came close to a League and FA Cup double, finally won him England recognition when he made his full international debut against Scotland. Just over a year later, he formed a crucial partnership alongside skipper Bobby Moore in England's 1966 World Cup-winning team and eventually won 35 caps for his country.

Although assured on the field Charlton was superstitious and relinquished the Leeds captaincy because of his liking to leave the dressing room last! Although not the most stylish of defenders, Big Jack would crane his neck to dominate in the air and used his telescopic stride to make long tackles; attributes that saw him dubbed 'the giraffe'. His consistent performances brought him the 1967 Footballer of the Year award.

In every game opposing forwards knew they would face a stern task and opposing goalkeepers and defenders also feared him, especially at set pieces, because he caused havoc when standing on their goal line. The number of goals he scored for a defender was phenomenal, 95 in all competitions. Notching his first against Blackburn Rovers in April 1959, many of his goals came from Charlton's tremendous heading ability, including a brace against Napoli in 1966 and the winner against Tottenham Hotspur in an FA Cup sixth round clash in 1972.

After numerous near-misses, Charlton claimed League Cup, First Division, FA Cup and Fairs Cup winners' medals, and also appeared in two FA Cup finals and a Fairs Cup final during Leeds' rise to prominence. Twelve months after Leeds' FA Cup success, time finally caught up with this football legend and he retired as a player at the end of the 1972/73 season aged thirty-eight. With George and Jack Milburn arriving at the club in 1928 the link between the Milburn family and Leeds United lasted forty-five years.

It was time for a new challenge and, beginning his managerial career at Middlesbrough, Charlton made an immediate impact, winning the Manager of the Year award in 1973/74 after guiding his charges to the Second Division title. He enjoyed a successful spell at Sheffield Wednesday but a move to Newcastle United didn't work out. However, another challenge was soon on the horizon. Many pundits felt Charlton should have managed England, but the Football Association's loss was the Republic of Ireland's gain. The role on the international stage was perfect for his style of management and, during his tenure, Charlton guided the Republic to the 1988 European Championships, where they defeated England; the 1990 World Cup, where they reached the quarter-finals and the 1994 World Cup. After failing to guide the Republic to the 1996 European Championship finals, Charlton retired but was awarded the Freedom of Dublin.

In recent years, Jack Charlton has built a career as one of the most sought-after speakers at sporting dinners. A natural, his wit and wide range of anecdotal stories from four decades in the game makes compulsive listening. However, Leeds United supporters remember him for his deeds during the Revie era when he helped Leeds take on all-comers at home and abroad. A one-club player, Charlton played more league matches than any other Leeds United player (628), and his 773 appearances in all competitions is a feat matched only by Billy Bremner. In a career that spanned twenty-one years, Big Jack was a true legend in every sense of the word.

ALLAN CLARKE

ALLAN CLARKE was one of English football's most feared strikers during the late 1960s and early 1970s and entered Leeds United folklore when he scored the only goal of the 1972 FA Cup final. Nicknamed 'Sniffer' due to his instinctive goal-poaching ability, Clarke was top draw and renowned as one of Europe's most clinical finishers; his chilling efficiency when one-on-one with a goalkeeper extraordinary.

Born in Willenhall, 31 July 1946, Clarke was the most famous of five footballing brothers. He made his Walsall debut at sixteen before honing his skills alongside George Cohen and Johnny Haynes at Fulham. Clearly impressed, Leicester City paid a British record £150,000 for his services in May 1968 and, during a turbulent season, Clarke won the Man of the Match award in the FA Cup final before moving to Elland Road for another British record fee, £165,000. Clarke would be the final piece of Don Revie's great side.

His debut for Leeds was in the club's Charity Shield win over Manchester City; a week later he scored on his league debut against Tottenham Hotspur. Linking up with Mick Jones in attack, they formed a formidable partnership, terrorising opposing defences wherever they played. Few bettered the Clarke-Jones partnership, and if that wasn't sufficient, 'Hotshot' Lorimer was supporting them!

At the end of the 1969/70 season, which saw Leeds nearly pull off a unique treble, Clarke scored a penalty on his full England debut against Czechoslovakia during the World Cup finals in Mexico. Carrying on his superb form in 1970/71, he scored in the final of the Fairs Cup against Juventus, winning his first major honour as a player. In 1971/72, Leeds played breathtaking football, but for Clarke and Leeds supporters one memory stands out, his flying header in the centenary FA Cup final against Arsenal, when he again won the Man of the Match award.

Clarke was at the peak of his career and, following the club's cup final disappointments in 1973, finally gained a league championship medal in 1973/74 after finishing a runner-up on three occasions. Although not his most prolific term as a goalscorer, he did score the winning goal in the penultimate game of the season; an incredibly tense affair at home to Ipswich Town that finished 3-2. The result ultimately clinched the title.

Following Don Revie's departure in the close season, one challenge remained for his former players, the European Cup. During a memorable campaign, Clarke scored a crucial goal against Barcelona in the semi-finals to help Leeds reach the final but tragically, Europe's premier trophy eluded them. As Revie's legends moved on, Clarke teamed up with Joe Jordan and Duncan McKenzie. Although no longer title contenders, Leeds were unlucky not to win any silverware, falling at the semi-final stage of the FA Cup and League Cup. Following knee surgery in 1977, Clarke knew his playing days at the top level were ending, but not before notching his 150th Leeds goal against Middlesbrough in 1978.

An England regular in the early 1970s, Clarke scored 10 goals in 19 appearances, and struck in some memorable encounters including when England defeated Austria 7-0 and Scotland 5-0. He also scored during England's infamous World Cup exit to Poland in 1973 following a 1-1 draw.

In an era when defences offered few opportunities, Clarke's speed off the mark and instant touch gave him a split second to cause damage, but he was also adept at harrying opponents into errors. Clarke's finishing ability set him apart. An assassin, he could waltz around a goalkeeper with nonchalant ease, catch a defender for pace, or place a shot or header into the net with deadly accuracy. A marksman of the highest calibre, he would punish every mistake by a defender.

Prior to the start of the 1978/79 season, Clarke joined Barnsley as player-manager. After leading them to promotion, he returned to manage Leeds in September 1980. Supporters welcomed Clarke's return but, in trying circumstances, his key signings, such as Peter Barnes at £930,000, failed to produce the goods. During a traumatic campaign in 1981/82 Leeds lost their fight for survival on the last day of the season. Clarke went on to guide Scunthorpe United before returning for a second spell with Barnsley, experiencing promotion, relegation, and numerous giant-killing acts in cup competitions before retiring from the game.

Still a regular visitor to Elland Road, Clarke always receives a terrific reception. The club's Player of the Year in 1972/73, Sniffer was top scorer for Leeds United on four occasions and is the club's third-highest goalscorer with 151 goals in 385 appearances; the abiding memory is his historic header at Wembley in 1972.

TERRY COOPER

TERRY COOPER began his playing career as an out-and-out winger before converting to a swashbuckling left-back on a regular basis at the start of the 1967/68 campaign. Within two years, Cooper was world class, his pace enabling him to support the attack with devastating effect.

Born in Brotherton, 12 July 1944, Cooper joined Leeds' rich crop of youngsters as an apprentice in 1961 and made his debut during the 1963/64 Second Division campaign. His opening games were a baptism of fire. On his debut against Swansea City, Leeds clinched promotion; on his second appearance at Charlton Athletic, the team clinched the title!

On his occasional appearances during the next three years, Cooper got used in crucial matches as a replacement for left-winger Albert Johanneson or left-back Willie Bell. Memorable call-ups included FA Cup semi-final clashes against Manchester United and Chelsea, and both legs of the club's first European final against Dynamo Zagreb. He also notched his first goal for the club at Aston Villa in August 1965, a campaign when he scored 4 goals in all competitions, his best return in a season.

The 1967/68 campaign finally saw Cooper make his mark in the number three shirt. A keen tackler, tactically astute and possessing natural pace, Cooper developed a tremendous understanding with Eddie Gray on the left flank. His experience as a winger helped him in his role as an overlapping full-back who could set up chances for his strikers with pinpoint crosses, and he was also able to anticipate his opponents' thoughts when defending as a former winger. Playing alongside Paul Reaney, Jack Charlton and Norman Hunter, Revie now had a balanced defence that would become the most reliable around.

In a memorable League Cup run, Cooper scored one goal. But what a crucial strike it was – the winner against Arsenal in the final at Wembley, the club's first 'major' honour. Within months, Leeds had claimed the Fairs Cup, following an aggregate win over Hungarian giants Ferencvaros. Cooper could not have timed his elevation to the first team better.

A key member of the First Division title-winning team in 1968/69, Cooper helped Leeds defeat Manchester City in the Charity Shield before playing his part in the club's 'treble' bid in 1969/70. For Cooper though there would be no rest after the FA Cup final defeat to Chelsea, because he was a regular for his country, having made his debut for England in a 5-0 win over France in March 1969. Within days, he was flying off to the World Cup finals in Mexico, a tournament acknowledged as the greatest football spectacle ever. His performances in the competition, especially against Brazil in the qualifying section, would see him become recognised as the best left-back in the world. Some accolade!

Carrying on his superb form into the 1970/71 season, though Leeds lost out in the race for the First Division title to Arsenal, his displays against Juventus in the Fairs Cup final triumph enhanced his reputation as the best left-back around. With the football world seemingly at his feet, tragically he broke a leg at Stoke City a week before Leeds' FA Cup semi-final win over Birmingham City in 1972. The injury sidelined him for nearly two years.

Although Cooper played a few more games for Leeds during the 1973/74 and 1974/75 campaigns, and made his twentieth and final appearance for England, he was unable to recapture his previous form. With Trevor Cherry in the side, Cooper's career at Leeds was over after fourteen seasons. Following spells at Middlesbrough and Bristol City, Cooper held coaching and managerial posts at Bristol Rovers, Doncaster Rovers, Bristol City, Exeter City (guiding them to the Fourth Division title in 1989/90) and Birmingham City. Today, he works as a European scout for Southampton.

A wonderfully talented footballer, Terry Cooper made 351 appearances, scoring 11 goals for Leeds United, the most notable his terrific goal at Wembley in 1968. The finest left-back the club has produced, T.C. was simply world class.

JOHNNY GILES

JOHNNY GILES was a central figure in Don Revie's legendary Leeds side for more than a decade following his arrival at Elland Road in August 1963. One of the great midfield generals of his era, Giles possessed exceptional passing ability, was a master tactician, scored his share of goals and could mix it with the best!

Born in Dublin, 6 January 1940, Giles developed at a number of local clubs, including Home Farm, before moving to England in 1957 to serve his apprenticeship at Manchester United. An FA Cup winner in 1963, when Giles failed to agree terms with Matt Busby during the close season he dropped down a division to join Revie at Leeds for £33,000. His signing would be one of the finest in the club's history.

Initially an outside right for Leeds, Giles arrived at the club feeling he had something to prove and played his part throughout the race for promotion in

1963/64. Missing only two games, his goal at Swansea helped secure top-flight football, the title confirmed in the last game at Charlton. Buoyed with confidence, the team astonished everyone in 1964/65 by finishing runners-up in both the league and FA Cup. Though a heartbreaking end, supporters knew an exciting era had dawned at the club.

Just weeks into the 1965/66 season Revie switched Giles into central midfield following an horrific injury to skipper Bobby Collins during a Fairs Cup tie against Torino. The astute Irishman's eye for a killer pass over any distance was soon apparent and he and Billy Bremner complemented each other brilliantly. Giles was not as volatile as Bremner, but possessed the same determination and will-to-win as his skipper and, in the heat of battle, Giles could be ruthless in his tackling. Orchestrating proceedings from the centre of the park Bremner and Giles became the most feared midfield partnership in the game.

Giles' ratio of goals from midfield was exceptional, scoring 115 in all competitions. A terrific striker of the ball, Giles hit double figures on five occasions during a season. Top scorer in 1966/67 with 18 goals, his most prolific campaign was 1969/70 when he scored 19. Although he was capable of striking from any distance, Giles became renowned as a penalty expert. His accuracy and composure made him the ideal choice and he rarely missed. Succeeding Willie Bell, Giles scored his first penalty for Leeds against Birmingham City in November 1964. Ever reliable, his best penalty haul was eight in 1969/70 and 1970/71, one short of Jack Milburn's record of nine spot kicks in 1935/36. Giles would score 44 goals from penalties over nine seasons, more than any other Leeds player.

Dubbed the 'Penalty King' by the *Yorkshire Evening Post*, Giles came up trumps during crucial cup ties, some of the most notable pressure spot kicks coming in European quarter-final matches against Bologna, Rangers, Standard Liege and Vitoria Setubal, and a League Cup semi-final clash against Derby County. On each occasion, Leeds won on aggregate. During the 1972/73 campaign Giles became only the second Leeds player to score a penalty in three consecutive league games (*v.* Sheffield United, West Brom and Ipswich Town), matching Milburn's feat in 1935/36.

When Don Revie became England manager in 1974, he recommended Giles as his successor at Leeds but the board ignored his advice. Within twelve months, Giles would also move on, but not before a final appearance at Wembley in the Charity Shield and another European Cup campaign, but the ultimate prize would elude Leeds.

Throughout an incredible era, Giles helped Leeds win the First Division championship and Fairs Cup twice, the FA Cup, League Cup and Charity Shield. He also played in three FA Cup finals, two European finals and was a First Division runner-up on five occasions. Despite the disappointments, Leeds won every domestic honour and were the team to beat every season.

His form naturally brought international recognition. After playing his first full international for the Republic of Ireland at eighteen, a record at the time, Giles went on to captain his country on many occasions, eventually winning 59 caps.

Within weeks of the European Cup final defeat in Paris, Giles began a successful spell as player-manager at West Brom. Guiding his players to promotion from the Second Division at the first attempt, he created one of the most attractive teams in the First Division before returning to Ireland in 1977 to manage Shamrock Rovers, where he won the FAI Cup. He then took up posts at Philadelphia Fury and Vancouver Whitecaps, before managing the Republic of Ireland and finally West Brom for a second spell.

Since his departure from The Hawthorns in 1985, Giles has developed a fresh career as an accomplished speaker on the after-dinner circuit, in addition to writing a regular football column for the *Daily Express*. Eighth on the all-time list at Leeds United with 527 appearances, Johnny Giles was one of the greatest footballers to represent the club.

EDDIE GRAY

EDDIE GRAY was one of the most sought-after youngsters in the country when he joined Leeds United in January 1965. A prodigious talent, and blessed with unbelievable ball skills, Eddie was a majestic sight with his darting runs down the left flank. His turning down his boyhood team Celtic for Leeds, like younger brother Frank some years later, says much for Don Revie's persuasive talents and vision for the club.

Born in Glasgow, 17 January 1948, Eddie scored on his league debut against Sheffield Wednesday on New Year's Day 1966, aged seventeen. By the end of the season, he had cemented his place in the first team and proceeded to tease, torment and bamboozle the best defenders in the First Division and Europe. A member of the Leeds side that won the League Cup in 1968 and the First Division title a year later, Eddie reserved one of his greatest exhibitions of wing-play for the 1970 FA Cup final. His virtuoso performance was even more remarkable due to the horrendous surface at Wembley that year following the Horse of the Year show and heavy rain. His efforts deservedly won him the Man of the Match award. Following his incredible display at Wembley, the world was at his feet, but injuries were beginning to take their toll and luck was certainly against him, especially in Europe. Over the years in the Fairs Cup, injuries dashed his hopes of playing in a semi-final play-off against Real Zaragoza, the second leg of finals against Dynamo Zagreb and Ferencvaros and, in 1971, an awkward fall in the abandoned first leg of the Fairs Cup final against Juventus forced him to miss Leeds' eventual triumph.

As with his club career, injuries affected Eddie's international career. Having represented Scotland at Schoolboy and Under-23 level, a full Scottish cap followed against England in the 1969 Home International Championships, but the 12 caps he eventually won were spread over seven seasons. One can only wonder what the world media would have written about Scotland at the 1974 World Cup finals if Eddie Gray had been fully fit.

Astonishingly, only once during the 1970s did Eddie play two-thirds of a league campaign, but thankfully he was able to take his place in many high-profile matches, especially during the club's treble bid in 1969/70 and he was present when Leeds celebrated their FA Cup triumph in 1972. Twelve months later he played in the FA Cup final against Sunderland, before the European jinx struck again, forcing him to miss the 1973 European Cup Winners' Cup final. After coming though pre-season training, Eddie missed the majority of the 1973/74 season, before fighting his way back in time to make an appearance in the 1975 European Cup final. Thereafter, Eddie finally experienced an injury-free run through the late 1970s. Playing for a number of managers, he once again thrilled supporters, scoring his only hat-trick against Leicester City in 1978. Brother Frank also scored, one of only four occasions the two did so for Leeds in a game. Although Leeds failed to win any silverware, they did reach three cup semi-finals and qualified for Europe in 1978/79.

Converting to left-back in 1980 added three years to his playing career, but his experience failed to prevent Leeds slipping into the Second Division after eighteen seasons of top-flight football. Replacing Allan Clarke as manager, Eddie began the complicated task of rebuilding the team with falling gates and little money. Blooding a number of promising apprentices during the 1982/83 season, results began to improve but it was a thankless task.

After three years at the helm, his twenty-year association with the club ended. Supporters were outraged, but he departed with dignity. A number of his youngsters, most notably John Sheridan, Scott Sellars and Denis Irwin, went on to have fine careers, justifying his faith in them. Eddie had not only witnessed the club's rise from First Division start-ups to one of European football's most respected teams, but had also witnessed the club's decline to Second Division minnows. His days at Leeds, however, were not quite over!

Resuming his playing career at non-league Whitby Town, Eddie finally retired in March 1986. Following a coaching role at Middlesbrough and managerial posts at Rochdale, Hull City and Whitby Town, Leeds United's prodigal son returned in 1995 as youth team coach. Under his tutelage the class of 1997 won the FA Youth Cup, the reserves clinched the Pontins League Division One title for the first time in sixty-one years and numerous youngsters that he nurtured, such as Harry Kewell, Jonathon Woodgate, Paul Robinson and Alan Smith, developed into international players.

Promoted to the first-team set-up in recent years, Eddie endured a roller-coaster ride as the finances of the club spiralled out of control. From Champions League contenders, Leeds were soon fighting for Premiership survival and, as a succession of managers departed, Eddie took the helm in a desperate bid to stave off relegation during the 2003/04 campaign. An impossible task, it surprised few supporters that his attempts failed and, when the inevitable occurred, his dignified departure demonstrated what the club meant to him.

Eddie will be remembered for his football skills, and rightly so, because he is the most naturally gifted player to represent Leeds United. In his distinctive style, Eddie could beat players for pace on the outside or inside, and although not renowned as a prolific goalscorer, among his 68 goals were a thirty-five-yard lob and unbelievable solo effort against Burnley in 1970 that are acknowledged as being among the greatest goals ever witnessed at Elland Road. On his day, Eddie was unstoppable, and when on song no defender in the world was safe. Seventh on the all-time appearances list at Leeds having played 579 games, Eddie Gray was a sensational player.

DAVID HARVEY

DAVID HARVEY made his Leeds United debut in a League Cup clash against West Brom in October 1965. At seventeen, the teenager was at the start of a brilliant career but had to be content with being Gary Sprake's understudy for seven years, playing 200 games for the reserves and 38 for the first team. Harvey would go on to become one of the club's greatest ever goalkeepers.

Born in Leeds, 7 February 1948, nobody could have blamed Harvey if he had decided to join another side; where he would have undoubtedly been first choice, but he didn't, which says much for Don Revie's man-management skills in keeping fringe players happy. His dedication would eventually pay off over a seventeen-year career.

Harvey was an incredibly hard trainer and put himself through the most punishing of schedules to develop his skills. Whenever called upon, whatever the occasion, he never let the team down. Notable appearances included Fairs Cup quarter-final clashes against Rangers and Vitoria Setubal, a European Cup semi-final encounter v. Celtic at Hampden Park, and a few days later an FA Cup final replay against Chelsea.

The turning point in his career followed a majestic display at Stoke City in April 1972. With the next fixture an FA Cup semi-final against Birmingham City, Revie had a massive decision to make. Should he retain Harvey or bring back Sprake, his more experienced keeper? On the morning of the match, Harvey won the vote.

Who knows what Revie's thought process was, but maybe he had finally decided that, for all Sprake's natural ability, he could not risk any more costly errors in high-profile matches. Harvey's calm display vindicated Revie's decision and in the final at

Wembley, a faultless performance in the triumph over Arsenal, sealed his position as the number-one choice.

Composed, determined and courageous, Harvey soon won international recognition through his consistent performances for Leeds, making his Scottish debut against Denmark in November 1972. As for his first full campaign, after being stretched off in an opening day defeat at Chelsea, he quickly recovered and helped Leeds reach the FA Cup and European Cup Winners' Cup finals. Although neither trophy would be won, Leeds began the 1973/74 league campaign with an incredible 29-game unbeaten run, and during a memorable campaign clinched the First Division title with a game to spare. To cap a great season, Harvey played in the 1974 World Cup finals in West Germany. Though Scotland failed to get beyond the initial group stages, his sensational performances against Brazil, Yugoslavia and Zaire resulted in him winning an award for being the best goalkeeper in the tournament. Harvey would go on to win 16 caps for Scotland.

Following Don Revie's departure, Harvey missed the vital spot kick against Liverpool in the club's Charity Shield defeat at Wembley. After Jimmy Armfield replaced Brian Clough as manager, an horrific car crash mid-season ended his campaign prematurely. Thereafter, Harvey would remain first choice, bar the odd spell out through injury, during a decade that saw two more managers at the club.

It was always going to be an uphill task following the Revie era, but new stars such as Duncan McKenzie, Tony Currie and Arthur Graham did well in extremely difficult circumstances. Although Leeds failed to win any silverware during the late 1970s they reached three cup semi-finals and qualified for Europe once again.

Harvey decided to move on in 1980 and, during a three-year spell, played for the Canadian side Vancouver Whitecaps and Drogheda in Ireland. In 1983 at the request of Eddie Gray, he returned to Elland Road following the departure of John Lukic to add vital experience to Gray's young team in the Second Division. Acting as skipper for two seasons, Harvey helped nurture the likes of John Sheridan, Tommy Wright and Scott Sellers, before finally severing links with the club in 1985 after 447 appearances. Following a brief spell with Bradford City he retired from the game.

It could not have been easy during the late 1960s and early 1970s for Harvey to watch Leeds season after season take on all comers at home and abroad. That he did and waited for his opportunity says much about his character. Although Leeds United won six major honours during the Revie era, others escaped. David Harvey was a first-class goalkeeper and one can only wonder what additional trophies Leeds might won had they benefited from his calming influence in the side earlier.

NORMAN HUNTER

NORMAN HUNTER was renowned during the 1960s and 1970s as one of the 'hard' men of the game alongside the likes of Ron Harris of Chelsea, Dave Mackay of Spurs and Nobby Stiles of Manchester United. A ferocious tackler and a colossus in defence, Hunter was an integral part of Don Revie's legendary team and one of the great personalities of British football.

Born in Eighton Banks, County Durham, 24 October 1943, Hunter joined Leeds as an apprentice in November 1960. Early on in the 1962/63 season, Revie decided to introduce the first of his talented youngsters and Hunter was one of those chosen when Leeds faced Swansea Town in September 1962. By the end of the campaign, Hunter was a fixture in the side and even scored his first goals for the club, against Middlesbrough and Charlton Athletic, where he scored the winning goal in a 2-1 win.

One of the pre-season favourites for promotion in 1963/64, Leeds clinched the title in the final game of the season. Hunter was the only ever-present in the side and again notched 2 goals, against Middlesbrough and Swindon Town. Following the Second Division title success, Hunter experienced all the highs and lows of the Revie era as Leeds took on all comers domestically and in Europe.

The only Leeds player to appear in every major final between 1965 and 1975, Hunter was ever-present during both First Division Championship triumphs. He won the Fairs Cup twice, and FA Cup, League Cup and Charity Shield winners' medals, and featured in Fairs Cup, European Cup Winners' Cup, European Cup finals, and three FA Cup finals. Hunter was also a regular in the side that finished First Division runners-up on no fewer than five occasions during an amazing era.

Over the years, Hunter's level of consistency was phenomenal and his value to the team immeasurable. However, his tackling ability became his trademark and you had to feel sympathy for a forward challenging him for a 50-50 ball. At times, some challenges looked brutal but he would never aim to hurt another player, though AC Milan pushed him to the limit in 1973! Naturally, he did have the odd spat on the pitch, most notably with Francis Lee in his Derby County days when the pair were sent off.

The club's Player of the Year in 1971 and PFA Player of the Year in 1973, Hunter is arguably the fiercest competitor to represent Leeds but there was much more to his game than just being an effective stopper. Quick, totally committed and blessed with great positional awareness, Hunter could slice a defence open with a long raking pass, play his way out of defence with consummate ease, support the attack brilliantly (as he demonstrated against Southampton in 1972 when making a goal for Charlton), and pack a thunderous shot, as numerous goalkeepers found out.

Of his 21 goals for Leeds, Hunter's only strike in the FA Cup came in the infamous 3-2 defeat at Colchester United in 1971. He enjoyed his most prolific season in 1965/66, notching 5 goals, including the only goal of the season's opener against Sunderland and a brace against West Ham in a 5-0 win.

Developing a superb understanding alongside Jack Charlton, Paul Reaney and Willie Bell, replaced by Terry Cooper in 1967, Hunter was part of a defensive unit that could handle the best strikers around. During his final three seasons at Leeds, Hunter formed a fine partnership alongside Gordon McQueen in the centre of defence. However, after sixteen years at Elland Road, Hunter was one of the first of Revie's legends to depart, joining Bristol City in 1976. After a three-year spell, Hunter joined Barnsley as player-coach, becoming manager when Allan Clarke departed to Leeds in 1980. Retiring as a player, Hunter guided the Tykes to promotion in his first season at the helm prior to holding posts at West Brom, Rotherham, Leeds and Bradford City.

For England, having won 3 caps for the Under-23s, Hunter made history on his full debut against Spain, when he became the first England player to be capped as a substitute. Playing in defence or occasionally midfield, he won 28 full caps, scoring twice. In many ways, Hunter was unlucky because he competed for a place against the great Bobby Moore, which meant he won far less caps than his ability deserved. Nevertheless a member of the 1966 and 1970 World Cup squads, playing in the classic quarter-final clash with West Germany, Hunter gave everything for his country. Of his international appearances, unfortunately the most memorable one was an infamous clash against Poland in 1973. The Polish goal was a nightmare, but the media treated him harshly for his missed tackle in the build-up. Hunter also made 6 appearances for the Football League and played in the Common Market Celebration match in 1973.

In recent years, this popular character has become a regular on the after-dinner circuit and an accomplished football pundit on BBC Radio Leeds. Playing more European ties than any other Leeds player (78), Hunter made 726 appearances for Leeds with Bremner, Charlton and Reaney ahead of him on the all-time list. In an astonishing career, after making his debut in 1962, Hunter featured in 439 of 462 league games. A magnificent footballer, Norman 'Bites yer Legs' Hunter was a tremendous servant and a legend at Leeds United.

MICK JONES

MICK JONES joined Leeds United in September 1967 for a club-record fee of £100,000. Totally unselfish, Jones grabbed his share of goals but it was his non-stop running for the benefit of the team that made him invaluable, a handful for defenders and a vital member of Don Revie's legendary side.

Born in Worksop, 24 April 1945, as a youngster Jones scored fourteen goals in a match for his school team. After playing for Worksop and Rotherham Boys, he joined Sheffield United in 1962 at seventeen and, during five years, scored 63 goals in 149 appearances. Capped at Under-23 level, he made 2 appearances for the full England team on a summer tour of Scandinavia in 1965.

Jones's move to Leeds gave Revie's team a cutting edge. Following his debut against Leicester City, Jones quickly established himself in the side and he notched his first Leeds goal in his European bow against Spora Luxembourg. Leeds' 9-0 win was a club record at the time. A niggling injury meant a spell on the sidelines but he was soon proving his potential on his return with a fine goal against Wolves and a brace in a comprehensive 5-0 victory at Fulham.

Jones duly claimed his first major honour when he scored the only goal of the delayed Fairs Cup final against Ferencvaros at the start of the 1968/69 season. In the league, after scoring in the opening three games of the season, he ended his first full campaign top scorer with 14 goals as Leeds claimed the First Division title. Notable winners came against Liverpool, at Sunderland and QPR, and two important strikes during the run-in at Arsenal and at home to Leicester City.

During the close season, Allan Clarke arrived at the club, which proved a masterstroke as Jones now had the perfect foil for his talents. From their first game together in the Charity Shield against Manchester City, the Clarke-Jones partnership clicked. The duo would become renowned at home and abroad as one of the finest in Europe and, with Peter Lorimer and Eddie Gray supporting from the flanks as an attacking force, no team was safe.

Jones used his strength to maximum effect in every game, whether shielding the ball, chasing lost causes or causing havoc in the penalty area before laying off a ball for his colleagues. He was also superb in the air and packed a fine shot. Enjoying his most prolific season in 1969/70, Jones opened the campaign with a brilliant headed winner at Manchester United and scored his first Leeds hat-trick in a club record 10-0 win against Lyn Oslo in the European Cup. By the end of a titanic campaign, the strike duo had scored 26 goals apiece as Leeds chased the treble. However, in a traumatic finale, Leeds ended the season with nothing, despite Jones giving Leeds the lead in both the FA Cup final and the replay against Chelsea. The season brought Jones his third England cap, against Holland in 1970, but mysteriously the best partnership domestically never played together on the international stage.

Over the next four seasons 'Jonah' was at his peak as Leeds won the FA Cup (Jones crossing the ball for Clarke's winner), another Fairs Cup title and a second First Division crown, when again he top scored with 14 goals. Among some distinguished performances in 1973/74, Jones scored the only goal of a tight encounter with Liverpool, a brace against West Ham and the opener in a 2-0 win at Old Trafford. Jones also helped Leeds reach two FA Cup finals, a European Cup Winners' Cup final and played his part as Leeds finished runners-up in the First Division on three occasions.

As the target man, Jones endured cynical punishment and, tragically, a bad knee injury midway through the second title campaign ultimately ended his playing career in October 1975. Indeed, his final game for Leeds was the penultimate match of the 1974 campaign against Ipswich Town, a game that ultimately clinched the title.

The abiding memory of Mick Jones for many Leeds United supporters is Wembley 1972 when, with his arm in a sling, he was determined to receive his winners' medal from the Queen in the Royal Box. The seventh highest scorer for the club with 111 goals in 313 appearances, Jones was top scorer on three occasions, and arguably his most memorable display was when he grabbed a hat-trick against Manchester United in 1972, only the second Leeds player to do so. The club's Player of the Year in his final season, Jones was the ideal target man.

JOE JORDAN

JOE JORDAN began his career at Morton in 1968. Recommended to Leeds United by his teammate and former Leeds legend Bobby Collins, Don Revie signed the raw teenage striker for £15,000 in October 1970. Jordan would terrorise the best defenders in world football.

Born in Carluke, Lanarkshire, 15 December 1951, Jordan initially replaced Mick Jones or Allan Clarke, when either was injured, but such was his progress Rod Belfitt departed. The youngster scored on his full Leeds debut against Barcelona in a Fairs Cup play-off match in 1971 and, over the next three seasons during sporadic runs in the first team, got used to more crucial matches, playing in the semi-final and final of the European Cup Winners' Cup in 1973.

Jordan finally got his break in 1973/74 and helped Leeds secure the First Division title. Never letting the team down, he scored some crucial goals, notably a late equaliser at Birmingham City and two great strikes against Arsenal.

Already a Scottish international, Jordan became a national hero in October 1973 when he scored a brilliant goal against Czechoslovakia to book his country's place at the 1974 World Cup finals. Though Scotland failed to get beyond the initial group stages, Jordan played superbly against Zaire, Brazil and Yugoslavia, scoring twice.

Following Don Revie's departure, Jordan began the 1974/75 season in the first team. Playing against Liverpool in the Charity Shield at Wembley, Jordan led the line as Leeds reached the European Cup final. As the likes of Bremner, Hunter, Jones and Giles moved on, Jimmy Armfield introduced Duncan McKenzie and Tony Currie alongside Jordan, Gordon McQueen and Frank Gray, and during the mid-1970s Leeds were unlucky not to win silverware, falling at the semi-finals of the FA Cup in 1977.

A regular for club and country, Jordan was utterly fearless and an awesome sight in full flow, his direct running intimidating opponents. Tremendously strong in the air, he excelled at laying a ball off or shielding a ball until a colleague was better placed. Defenders wound him up, but Jordan was capable of looking after himself!

A few months into the 1977/78 campaign, Jordan shocked Leeds supporters by joining arch-rivals Manchester United for a club-record fee of £350,000. It was a massive blow to Leeds, but not to Jordan's career. After appearing in the 1978 World Cup finals, when again he scored, he enhanced his reputation during three seasons at Old Trafford, helping them to the 1979 FA Cup final. In 1981, Jordan joined Italian giants AC Milan, before playing in a third World Cup. Scoring against New Zealand made him the only Scot to score in three consecutive finals. Jordan gained 52 caps for his country. Following a season at Verona, this cracking old-fashioned style centre forward joined Southampton for £100,000 in 1984. Joining Bristol City, Jordan helped them win the Freight/Rover Trophy in 1987. Appointed player-manager, he steered City to a League Cup semi-final in 1988/89 and promotion to the Second Division the following year. Since then, he has held a number of managerial and coaching posts at Hearts, Celtic, Stoke City, Bristol City again, Northern Ireland and Huddersfield Town. Currently he is a coach at Portsmouth.

For all his successes, Joe Jordan played some of his best football at Leeds United. Scoring 48 goals in 221 appearances, Jordan was top scorer in 1976/77 and the perfect replacement for Mick Jones. Playing more games for Leeds than for his future clubs, Leeds supporters saw the development of a fantastic talent.

PETER LORIMER

PETER LORIMER is the most prolific goalscorer in Leeds United's history. Records are set to be broken but his tally of 238 goals in all competitions, 81 more than the legendary John Charles, is surely beyond anyone.

Born in Dundee, 11 December 1946, Lorimer was a prodigious Schoolboy talent, scoring 176 goals one season! With numerous clubs chasing his signature, Don Revie worked tirelessly to add him to join his crop of youngsters at Elland Road. His efforts would be richly rewarded. Joining Leeds in May 1962, Lorimer became the club's youngest debutant when he faced Southampton aged fifteen years and 289 days but he didn't become a regular until the 1965/66 campaign. Opening his account in a 3-2 defeat at Tottenham Hotspur, Lorimer scored a brace in victories against Blackburn Rovers, Northampton Town and Nottingham Forest. He also grabbed his first hat-trick in an FA Cup tie against Bury and finished top scorer on 19 goals.

Leading scorer two years later with 30 goals, his highest total for Leeds, the 1967/68 campaign saw Leeds win the League Cup and Fairs Cup. Lorimer was leading scorer in both competitions and, among his European goals, four came against Spora Luxembourg in a club-record 9-0 win, and his strikes against Partizan Belgrade and Rangers proved crucial. In the league, Lorimer won clashes against Burnley, West Ham and Tottenham, and scored in Leeds' 7-0 win against Chelsea.

Leeds were at the height of their powers and, after winning the First Division title in 1968/69, only fixture congestion denied them more trophies the following term when they finished runners-up in all three major competitions. It was a bitter disappointment, but honours arrived in 1970/71 with the Fairs Cup. Lorimer top scored with 5 goals, including vital strikes against Dynamo Dresden and Vitoria Setubal. In 1971/72, Lorimer completed his domestic collection with an FA Cup winners' medal. His haul of 29 goals included a hat-trick in Leeds' 7-0 demolition of Southampton. The following campaign would be notable for Leeds missing out in both the FA Cup and European Cup Winners' Cup finals, but the lasting memory was Jim Montgomery's outrageous save from Lorimer at Wembley. Three decades on the Sunderland 'keeper's point-blank save still defies belief.

Twelve months on Leeds claimed another First Division crown, but made hard work of it after beginning the 1973/74 campaign with a 29-game unbeaten run. Although not his most prolific season, Lorimer grabbed a hat-trick against Birmingham City but his four goals in the run-in proved more crucial as Leeds came through a difficult spell. The relief following his strikes in 2-0 victories against Derby

County and Sheffield United and his goal in the 3–2 win over Ipswich Town was extraordinary. The latter result ultimately clinched the title.

Following Don Revie's departure during the close season, Jimmy Armfield eventually took the helm and, during a memorable European Cup campaign, Lorimer scored arguably his most crucial goal for Leeds against Barcelona to clinch a place in the final. His brilliant volley against Bayern Munich looked to have won the trophy but was ruled out because Billy Bremner had strayed offside. Alongside his last-minute free-kick against Chelsea in the 1967 FA Cup semi-final, both efforts are still the most debated disallowed goals in the club's history.

As former colleagues moved on, Leeds were no longer title contenders but were unlucky not to win silverware, falling at the semi-final stages of the FA Cup in 1977 and League Cup in 1978. After sixteen seasons at the club, Lorimer embarked on a five-year spell at Toronto Blizzards, Vancouver Whitecaps and York City before returning to Leeds in December 1983, following a request by ex-teammate Eddie Gray to help his former club who were languishing near the bottom of the Second Division.

Playing in midfield, Lorimer helped Leeds finish tenth and, on an historical note, finally overhauled John Charles's record of 153 league goals with a penalty against Oldham Althletic. Lorimer played his final game for Leeds against Grimsby Town in 1985 at the age of thirty-nine. Following a brief spell at Whitby and Hapoel Haifa, Lorimer retired after twenty-four seasons as a professional footballer.

Dubbed 'Hotshot' Lorimer, 'keepers domestically and in Europe grasped air on numerous occasions. When it came to free-kicks, Lorimer's prowess was legendary and he scored countless goals down the years. Dangerous from anywhere in an opponents' half, Lorimer once scored from the halfway line! His power made him a natural penalty expert, but he had to wait at Leeds because Johnny Giles was the undisputed number one. Nevertheless, after scoring his first spot kick against Preston North End in 1966, Lorimer scored 32 penalties, second only to Giles.

This remarkable player was not just a goalscorer though. Lorimer could spread play with superb accuracy, created many goals for Allan Clarke and Mick Jones with pinpoint crosses from the right flank and, blessed with poise and ball control, could take on the best full-backs around. On the international stage, Lorimer represented Scotland as an amateur prior to making his full Scottish debut in 1969 against Spain. Bizarrely, this clash came a month before his Under-23 debut against France! Following one more appearance for the Under-23s, Lorimer gained 21 caps for his country, scoring 4 goals. Among a number of memorable performances, Lorimer played in the 1974 World Cup finals, scoring a trademark volley against Zaire.

In recent years, Lorimer has become an accomplished radio summariser and returned to the club as a director in 2004. Extremely popular with supporters, Peter Lorimer is one of the club's greatest ever players. Sixth on the all-time list with 705 appearances, but for his spell away from the club he would have claimed this record on top of his goalscoring achievements. One of only four players alongside Tom Jennings, John Charles and Lee Chapman to score thirty goals in a season, for supporters the lasting memory of Peter Lorimer will be of him unleashing a thunderbolt during his heyday. There was no finer sight.

PAUL MADELEY

PAUL MADELEY joined Leeds United as an apprentice in 1961 and went on to become the most versatile player in the club's history during a seventeen-year career. Indeed, after making his debut against Manchester City in January 1964 as a replacement for Jack Charlton, such was his ability to play in different positions he was not regarded as simply a full-back, centre half or midfielder because he could play anywhere, and did.

Born in Leeds, 20 September 1944, Madeley had two nicknames: 'Mr Versatile' due to his flexibility, and 'Rolls Royce' because of the smooth manner in which he glided around a football field. Remarkably, Madeley appeared in every outfield position. Indeed, in 1966/67, Madeley wore every shirt bar number eleven!

One of the fittest players in the squad, despite not having a dedicated role in Revie's legendary team, Madeley was always in the starting XI whether due to an injury, suspension or tactical reasoning. This ability was vital to Leeds' success during the Revie era because he was able to slot into different positions at a moment's notice without affecting the balance of the side.

Analysing the roles Madeley played for Leeds, especially in finals, it is easy to understand why this remarkable player was so important to the team. Madeley holds the unique achievement of playing in four domestic finals at Wembley in four different positions: 1968 League Cup (centre forward); 1970 FA Cup (right-back); 1972 FA Cup (left-back) and 1973 FA Cup (centre half). In addition, Madeley played on the left side of midfield in the 1968 and 1971 Fairs Cup finals and the 1973 European Cup Winners' Cup final, and centre half in the 1975 European Cup final.

Not renowned as a goalscorer, Madeley scored the first of 34 goals for Leeds with a long-range strike at Leicester City in September 1965, before enjoying his most prolific season in 1967/68. Playing as an auxiliary striker for a period, apart from several others, Madeley notched 10 goals in all competitions. Scoring a brace against Southampton in a 5-0 win, Madeley struck in a club record 9-0 win against Spora Luxembourg and his header earned Leeds a 1-1 draw at Dundee during a Fairs Cup semi-final clash, Leeds winning the tie 2-1 on aggregate.

Three years on, colleagues dubbed him 'goal-a-game' Madeley after strikes against Blackpool, Stoke City and Wolves in consecutive games! However, the most important goal of his illustrious career came at the end of the 1970/71 campaign against Juventus in the first leg of the Fairs Cup final when Leeds won the trophy on away goals. Thereafter, goals were very much at a premium, Madeley's seventh in eight seasons securing a 4-0 win against Southampton in November 1978.

In an outstanding career, Madeley helped Leeds win the First Division championship and Fairs Cup twice, the FA Cup, League Cup and Charity Shield. He also featured in European Cup Winners' Cup, European Cup and two FA Cup finals, and played in First Division runners-up campaigns on no fewer than five occasions.

Following Don Revie's departure and the European Cup final defeat to Bayern Munich in 1974/75, as numerous colleagues moved on, Madeley played alongside Gordon McQueen and Paul Hart in central defence. Serving a number of managers in the late 1970s, although not title contenders, Leeds finished fifth in 1975/76 and 1978/79 and reached FA Cup and League Cup semi-finals.

On the international stage, Madeley hit the headlines when he dropped out of Sir Alf Ramsey's twenty-eight-man squad that was due to travel to the 1970 World Cup finals. Ramsey, however, understood Madeley's reasons and gave him his full debut in 1971. As with Leeds, Madeley represented his country in a variety of positions in defence or midfield, winning a total of 24 caps.

Madeley was world class in a number of positions. A ball-winner and playmaker, Madeley had great positional awareness, natural strength and was superb in the air. Of all the roles he filled, playing the defensive midfield role demonstrated his abilities best. His long stride enabled him to make ground quickly before playing a sweeping pass or a deft flick, and his tackles were crisp and immaculately timed.

Retiring in 1980, he joined the family's successful chain of home decor stores. Fifth on the all-time list following his 725 appearances for the club, Madeley played a club record 50 League Cup ties. A one-club player, Paul Madeley was priceless for Leeds United.

PAUL REANEY

PAUL REANEY enjoyed a tremendous career at Leeds United. Blessed with lightning pace, 'Speedy' Reaney was right-back throughout the Revie era as Leeds became the team to beat every season. A strong tackler, superb man-marker and possessing great positional awareness, Reaney was able to monitor the best wingers around. George Best noted during his career that his most difficult games were when facing Reaney. There can be no finer tribute.

Born in London, 22 October 1944, Reaney's family moved to Leeds when he was only a few weeks old. A fine sprinter and footballer, Reaney was an apprentice mechanic when he was asked to join the Leeds ground staff in October 1961. Inside a year Reaney, Gary Sprake and Norman Hunter were thrust into the first team at Swansea Town as Revie began the process of introducing his talented youngsters. Developing a great understanding alongside Willie Bell (replaced by Terry Cooper in 1967), Jack Charlton and Hunter, Leeds had a defensive unit that could cope with the best strikers in the game.

A key member of the team that claimed the Second Division title in 1963/64, Reaney would miss only seven league games up to the 1970 FA Cup final, when a broken leg sustained at West Ham United cost him a place at Wembley and a chance to play at the World Cup finals in Mexico. It was a devastating blow for Reaney, who had represented the Football League on 3 occasions, won 5 Under-23 caps and 2 full caps for England. After making a full recovery he won a third cap in 1971 but his total was a poor return for a player of his class.

Developing a great understanding with Peter Lorimer down the right flank, Reaney caused havoc for opposing defences with his teasing crosses. One of the fittest and most reliable right-backs of his generation, of all his attributes the one that he became renowned for was his goal-line clearances. It was an uncanny skill, but repeatedly Reaney came up trumps, appearing from nowhere to stop a certain goal. His most important clearance came during the FA Cup final triumph against Arsenal in 1972 when, in one of the game's pivotal moments Reaney cleared a certain goal from an Alan Ball strike in the first half.

Winning the First Division championship and Fairs Cup twice, the FA Cup, League Cup and Charity Shield, Reaney also played in two FA Cup finals and all three European finals, skippering the side against AC Milan in the European Cup Winners' Cup final due to the absence of Billy Bremner through suspension. During this period he was also part of the Leeds teams that finished First Division runners-up on five occasions.

A Reaney goal was a rarity. Scoring 9, he was a lucky talisman because following one of his goals Leeds never lost, drawing twice and winning seven. His first strike came against Stoke City in the FA Cup, but most memorably he scored against Manchester United in the final game of 1965/66 and the third match of 1966/67.

Following the departure of Don Revie, it was only a matter of time before Reaney moved on. After eighteen seasons at Leeds United, this legendary player decided to join Bradford City in June 1978 before ending his playing career at Newcastle UB United, where he was voted Australia's 'Player of the Year'.

In recent years, Reaney has run coaching clinics and remains involved at Elland Road as part of the corporate hospitality matchday team. Playing more FA Cup ties than any other Leeds United player (72), this phenomenal footballer made 736 appearances for the club, with only Bremner and Charlton ahead of him on the all-time list.

GARY SPRAKE

GARY SPRAKE made a dramatic entry to senior football for Leeds United at the age of sixteen when he was called on as a last-minute replacement for goalkeeper Tommy Younger against Southampton in March 1962. With the squad on the South Coast, Leeds' apprentice keeper flew down on the day of the match and only just made the kick-off. The match ended in a 4-1 defeat but Sprake was soon an ever-present as Don Revie began the process of producing Leeds United's greatest ever team.

Born in Winchwen, near Swansea, 3 April 1945, Sprake grew up close to legendary Welsh goalkeeper Jack Kelsey. A Schoolboy star, the budding 'keeper joined Leeds' band of youngsters at Elland Road being groomed for stardom. Turning professional two months after making his debut, Revie played Sprake, Paul Reaney and Norman Hunter at Swansea Town in September 1962. All three would become legends and, alongside Willie Bell (replaced by Terry Cooper in August 1967) and Jack Charlton, Leeds had a defensive unit that would cope with the best strikers around.

A key member of the 1963/64 side that secured the Second Division title, Sprake would be Revie's number-one keeper as Leeds claimed the First Division title with a record number of points in 1968/69, the League Cup in 1967/68 and the Fairs Cup twice in 1967/68 and 1970/71. The most consistent team around, Sprake was also in goal when Leeds finished runners-up in the league on five occasions, reached two FA Cup finals and a Fairs Cup final during a sensational period.

Generally Sprake was a model of consistency but he did make the occasional 'howler' in high-profile televised games. His most embarrassing clanger came at Anfield in 1966/67 when he threw the ball into his own net. The Liverpool Kop immediately sang *Careless Hands*! Against Everton in an FA Cup semi-final in 1967/68, his error cost the only goal of the game, as it did in the last minute of a league clash against Crystal Palace in 1970/71. However, Sprake's worst mistake came against Chelsea in the 1970 FA Cup final when, with Leeds in control, Sprake let in a soft equaliser just before the half-time interval.

The occasional lapse apart, Sprake was one of the best 'keepers around during the late 1960s and early 1970s. He needed to be because David Harvey was an outstanding deputy. Blessed with natural ability, Sprake anticipated trouble, was a terrific shot-stopper, often inspirational and won many games for Leeds. His best performance came in Budapest in the Fairs Cup final second leg against Ferencvaros when Leeds clinched the trophy for the first time. Sprake was outstanding and pulled off a number of world-class saves.

The watershed in Sprake's career came in 1971/72 when Revie preferred Harvey to his more experienced goalkeeper in the semi-finals of the FA Cup. As Leeds went on to claim the only domestic honour to elude them, Sprake was a non-playing reserve and realised his days at Leeds were over. Following a brief spell at Birmingham City, Sprake retired through injury in 1975.

On the international stage, Sprake became Wales' youngest keeper when he faced Scotland in 1964 aged eighteen and went on to win 37 caps over an eleven-year period. When evaluating his career at Leeds United, Gary Sprake had more good games than bad ones, but his lack of concentration at crucial moments cost Leeds dearly. Supporters will always wonder whether Leeds would have won more trophies had Revie switched Harvey and Sprake earlier, but the record books state that this talented Welshman played in goal for Leeds more than any other player and is one of only nine individuals to make 500 appearances for the club.

TERRY YORATH

TERRY YORATH signed professional forms with Leeds United at just seventeen but, like many youngsters at Elland Road, had to wait some years before cementing a place in the first team. Predominantly a tough-tackling midfield player, Yorath became a valuable member of the side in the mid-1970s that won a First Division championship.

Born Cardiff, 27 March 1950, Yorath was a promising rugby union player before he fortuitously played for Cardiff Boys when they were a player short. The outstanding player on the day, Yorath won 4 Welsh Schoolboy caps and, after turning down offers from Bristol Rovers, Bristol City and his hometown club Cardiff City, joined the Revie revolution at Leeds.

Following his debut against Burnley in May 1968, Yorath would not get an extended run in the first team until the final games of the 1969/70 season when the league campaign was over. Spasmodic appearances would follow until 1972/73 and, like so many of Revie's aces waiting in the wings, he did not disappoint when called up.

During the campaign, Yorath was outstanding when he came on for Jack Charlton in Leeds' FA Cup semi-final win against Wolves, and deputised in both legs of the European Cup Winners' Cup semi-final against Hajduk Split. Reaching two finals was a great achievement but both would end in heartache. Yorath featured in both, coming on for Eddie Gray in the FA Cup final against Sunderland and playing centre half against AC Milan in the European Cup Winners' Cup final in Salonika.

In many ways, Yorath had been extremely unfortunate because, having gained 8 caps, he would have walked into most First Division sides. Indeed, when Yorath made his Welsh debut against Italy in a World Cup qualifying match in November 1969, he had only played in the Leeds first team twice and made two substitute appearances!

In 1973/74, Yorath finally broke into the side following injuries initially to Eddie Gray, then Johnny Giles and to the Irishman's deputy Mick Bates. With Paul Madeley deputising for Gray, Yorath came in for Bates. In all Yorath played in five positions during the season, and impressed on the left side of midfield alongside Bremner and Madeley as Leeds powered their way to a second league title.

Yorath scored twice during the league campaign, at Ipswich and the only goal against Norwich City. Having won his first major honour, Yorath played throughout the 1974/75 campaign when Leeds reached the European Cup final. Unfortunately, as new boss Jimmy Armfield began the process of replacing Revie's legends, Yorath became the scapegoat for a section of home supporters' frustrations, even though he always gave his best whether playing in midfield, defence or as an auxiliary striker.

Joining Coventry City for £125,000 at the end of the 1975/76 season, after three seasons, Yorath played for Tottenham Hotspur, Bradford City and Swansea City, but injuries meant he would play less than 80 games in eight years. On the international scene, Yorath represented Wales for twelve years, winning 59 caps.

As a manager, Yorath guided a number of clubs, including Wales, who he so nearly took to the 1996 European Championships. Currently assistant manager at Huddersfield Town, his daughter Gabby Logan is a well-known media star but, sadly, tragedy struck the Yorath family when son Daniel died of a heart condition.

Underrated, Terry Yorath was a fine utility player and whenever called upon never let anyone down. Like Rod Belfitt, Terry Hibbitt and Mick Bates before him, Yorath was a testament to Revie's man-management skills and without players of his quality and loyalty, Leeds United would not have been the force they became.

Leeds United on Television

BBC *Match of the Day*

Leeds United featured twelve times on the popular soccer programme during the 1971/72 season. Manchester United appeared on thirteen shows, Arsenal eleven, Manchester City eight, Liverpool and Tottenham seven, while defending champions Derby County made six appearances.

16/10/1971	First Division	Leeds United 3	Manchester City 0
30/10/1971	First Division	Manchester United 0	Leeds United 1
11/12/1971	First Division	Chelsea 0	Leeds United 0
29/01/1972	First Division	Tottenham Hotspur 1	Leeds United 0
9/02/1972	FA Cup Fourth Rnd	Liverpool 0	Leeds United 0
19/02/1972	First Division	Leeds United 5	Manchester United 1
26/02/1972	FA Cup Fifth Rnd	Cardiff City 0	Leeds United 2
4/03/1972	First Division	Leeds United 7	Southampton 0
18/03/1972	FA Cup Sixth Rnd	Leeds United 2	Tottenham Hotspur 1
1/04/1972	First Division	Derby County 2	Leeds United 0
15/04/1972	FA Cup Semi-Final	Birmingham City 0	Leeds United 3
6/05/1972	FA Cup Final	Arsenal 0	Leeds United 1

FA Cup 1971/72 Statistics

Saturday 15 January 1972
Elland Road
Attendance: 33,565

LEEDS UNITED 4   BRISTOL ROVERS 1
Giles 17, 35 (pen)   Allen 73
Lorimer 23, 82

Leeds United: Gary Sprake, Paul Reaney, Terry Cooper, Billy Bremner, Paul Madeley, Norman Hunter, Peter Lorimer, Mick Bates, Joe Jordan, Johnny Giles, Eddie Gray. Sub: Chris Galvin (Jordan).

Bristol Rovers: Dick Sheppard, Phil Roberts, Lindsey Parsons, Frank Prince, Stuart Taylor, Brian Godfrey, Ken Stephens, Wayne Jones, Sandy Allen, Bruce Bannister, Peter Higgins. Sub: Tom Stanton (Jones).

Referee: Anthony Morrissey (Bramall)

Saturday 5 February 1972
Anfield
Attendance: 56,598

LIVERPOOL 0   LEEDS UNITED 0

Liverpool: Ray Clemence, Chris Lawler, Alec Lindsay, Tommy Smith, Larry Lloyd, Emlyn Hughes, Kevin Keegan, Ian Ross, Steve Heighway, John Toshack, Ian Callaghan. Sub: Bobby Graham.
Leeds United: Gary Sprake, Paul Reaney, Terry Cooper, Billy Bremner, Paul Madeley, Norman Hunter, Peter Lorimer, Allan Clarke, Mick Jones, Johnny Giles, Mick Bates. Sub: Terry Yorath.

Referee: Graham Hill (Leicester)

Wednesday 9 February 1972
Elland Road
Attendance: 45,821

LEEDS UNITED 2   LIVERPOOL 0
Clarke 22, 63

Leeds United: Gary Sprake, Paul Reaney, Terry Cooper, Billy Bremner, Jack Charlton, Norman Hunter, Peter Lorimer, Allan Clarke, Paul Madeley, Johnny Giles, Eddie Gray. Sub: Joe Jordan (Reaney).

Liverpool: Ray Clemence, Chris Lawler, Alec Lindsay, Tommy Smith, Larry Lloyd, Emlyn Hughes, Kevin Keegan, Ian Ross, Steve Heighway, Bobby Graham, Ian Callaghan. Sub: Phil Boersma (Heighway).

Referee: Graham Hill (Leicester)

Saturday 26 February 1972
Ninian Park
Attendance: 50,000

CARDIFF CITY 0   LEEDS UNITED 2
                      Giles 35, 84

Cardiff City: Bill Irwin, David Carver, Gary Bell, Billy Kellock, Don Murray, Leighton Phillips, Ian Gibson, Brian Clark, Peter King, Bobby Woodruff, Alan Foggan. Sub: Alan Warboys (Foggan).

Leeds United: Gary Sprake, Paul Madeley, Terry Cooper, Billy Bremner, Jack Charlton, Norman Hunter, Peter Lorimer, Allan Clarke, Mick Jones, Johnny Giles, Eddie Gray. Sub: Paul Reaney.

Referee: K. Walker (Ashford)

Saturday 18 March 1972
Elland Road
Attendance: 43,937

LEEDS UNITED 2   TOTTENHAM HOTSPUR 1
Clarke 44   Pratt 42
Charlton 52

Leeds United: Gary Sprake, Paul Madeley, Terry Cooper, Billy Bremner, Jack Charlton, Norman Hunter, Peter Lorimer, Allan Clarke, Mick Jones, Johnny Giles, Eddie Gray. Sub: Paul Reaney (Cooper).

Tottenham Hotspur: Pat Jennings, Ray Evans, Cyril Knowles, John Pratt, Mike England, Phil Beal, Alan Gilzean, Steve Perryman, Martin Chivers, Martin Peters, Roger Morgan. Sub: Ralph Coates (Peters).

Referee: Jack Taylor (Wolverhampton)

Saturday 15 April 1972
Hillsborough
Attendance: 55,000

BIRMINGHAM CITY 0 LEEDS UNITED 3
Jones 18, 64
Lorimer 24

Birmingham City: Paul Cooper, Tommy Carroll, Gary Pendrey, Malcolm Page, Roger Hynd, Stan Harland, Alan Campbell, Trevor Francis, Bob Latchford, Bob Hatton, George Smith. Sub: Gordon Taylor (Latchford).

Leeds United: David Harvey, Paul Reaney, Paul Madeley, Billy Bremner, Jack Charlton, Norman Hunter, Peter Lorimer, Allan Clarke, Mick Jones, Johnny Giles, Eddie Gray. Sub: Mick Bates.

Referee: Norman Burtenshaw (Great Yarmouth)

Saturday 6 May 1972
Wembley Stadium
Attendance: 100,000
Receipts: £191,197

ARSENAL 0   LEEDS UNITED 1
                   Clarke 53

Arsenal: Geoff Barnett, Pat Rice, Bob McNab, Peter Storey, Frank McLintock, Peter Simpson, George Armstrong, Alan Ball, John Radford, George Graham, Charlie George. Sub: Ray Kennedy (Radford).

Leeds United: David Harvey, Paul Reaney, Paul Madeley, Billy Bremner, Jack Charlton, Norman Hunter, Peter Lorimer, Allan Clarke, Mick Jones, Johnny Giles, Eddie Gray. Sub: Mick Bates.

Referee: David Smith (Gloucestershire)

Other Leeds United FC titles published by Tempus:

Leeds United's 'Rolls Royce' The Paul Madeley Story
DAVID SAFFER

Paul Madeley is one of the finest utility players in the history of the game. He featured in every outfield position for Leeds United and performed brilliantly in every one of them. ALthough versatile in terms of what position he played, he was rigid regarding who he would play for – Leeds United and his country. This is the enthralling story of a true professional.
0 7524 3071 8

The Life and Times of Mick Jones
DAVID SAFFER

Mick Jones burst onto the football scene with Sheffield United, making his debut just before his eighteenth birthday in 1963. Well-built, determined and hardworking, he was sold for a record fee to Leeds in 1967. Mick played a crucial role in the great Leeds side of the early 1970s. His partnership with Allan Clarke was one of the finest ever seen in the domestic game. This is the compelling official biography of one of the most feared strikers of the late 1960s and early '70s.
0 7524 2419 X

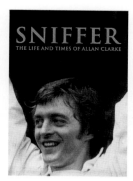

Sniffer The Life and Times of Allan Clarke
DAVID SAFFER

One of English football's great strikers, Allan Clarke was renowned home and abroad as one of the most clinical finishers around. He made his debut for Walsall aged sixteen and honed his skills at Fulham before British record transfers took him to Leicester City and then to Leeds where, under Revie, Clarke had his best years as a player, winning FA Cup, Championship and European honours. This lavishly illustrated biography is a celebration of a remarkable career.
0 7524 2168 9

Other Leeds United FC titles published by Tempus:

Leeds United FC Images of Sport
DAVID SAFFER & HOWARD DAPIN

Leeds United are one of the biggest and proudest football clubs in the world. This selection of significant memorabilia follows the club from its foundation in 1919 right up to the current exciting crop of youngsters. Included along the way are many special events, such as the Fairs Cup triumphs in 1968 and 1971, the League Championships of 1968/69, 1973/74 and 1991/92 and the 1972 FA Cup. With a foreword by Elsie Revie, this collection of over 200 images (including action shots, team group photographs, programme covers and cartoons) brings this rich sporting heritage to life.
0 7524 1642 1

Leeds Legends
DAVID SAFFER

From the formation of Leeds City in 1904 through their 1920 transformation into Leeds United and the many promotions, relegations, cups and championships that have followed, hundreds of players have worn the club shirt with pride. From loyal club stalwarts to controversial mavericks, many of these characters are worthy of being classed as true legends at Elland Road. Over 100 great names are featured in *Leeds Legends*, which contains detailed biographies, comprehensive statistics and an foreword by the late, great John Charles CBE.
0 7524 2700 8

Leeds United Champions 1991/92
DAVID SAFFER

It was the last season before the Premiership began and whoever topped the table would be the final 'proper' Champions of the Football League. When the 1991/92 campaign began, several clubs were in the running – among them an expensively assembled Leeds United team led by Howard Wilkinson. This is the story of how the side turned their potential into honours to be acclaimed as the best in the land for the third time in their history. Extensively illustrated and with detailed reports of every League game, it is an essential read for anyone who has an interest in Leeds United.
0 7524 3112 9